T0324911

Algorithmic Aspects of Machine Learning

This book bridges theoretical computer science and machine learning by exploring what the two sides can teach each other. It emphasizes the need for flexible, tractable models that better capture not what makes machine learning hard but what makes it easy. Theoretical computer scientists will be introduced to important models in machine learning and to the main questions within the field. Machine learning researchers will be introduced to cutting-edge research in an accessible format and will gain familiarity with a modern algorithmic toolkit, including the method of moments, tensor decompositions, and convex programming relaxations.

The treatment goes beyond worst-case analysis to build a rigorous understanding about the approaches used in practice and to facilitate the discovery of exciting new ways to solve important, long-standing problems.

ANKUR MOITRA is the Rockwell International Associate Professor of Mathematics at the Massachusetts Institute of Technology. He is a principal investigator in the Computer Science and Artificial Intelligence Lab (CSAIL) and a core member of the Theory of Computation Group, Machine Learning@MIT, and the Center for Statistics. The aim of his work is to bridge the gap between theoretical computer science and machine learning by developing algorithms with provable guarantees and foundations for reasoning about their behavior. He is the recipient of a Packard Fellowship, a Sloan Fellowship, a National Science Foundation CAREER Award, an NSF Computing and Innovation Fellowship, and a Hertz Fellowship.

To Diana and Olivia, the sunshine in my life

Algorithmic Aspects of Machine Learning

ANKUR MOITRA
Massachusetts Institute of Technology

CAMBRIDGE
UNIVERSITY PRESS

CAMBRIDGE
UNIVERSITY PRESS

University Printing House, Cambridge CB2 8BS, United Kingdom

One Liberty Plaza, 20th Floor, New York, NY 10006, USA

477 Williamstown Road, Port Melbourne, VIC 3207, Australia

314-321, 3rd Floor, Plot 3, Splendor Forum, Jasola District Centre, New Delhi - 110025, India

79 Anson Road, #06-04/06, Singapore 079906

Cambridge University Press is part of the University of Cambridge.

It furthers the University's mission by disseminating knowledge in the pursuit of education, learning and research at the highest international levels of excellence.

www.cambridge.org
Information on this title: www.cambridge.org/9781107184589
DOI: 10.1017/9781316882177

© Ankur Moitra 2018

First published 2018

A catalogue record for this publication is available from the British Library

Library of Congress Cataloging in Publication data
Names: Moitra, Ankur, 1985– author.
Title: Algorithmic aspects of machine learning / Ankur Moitra,
Massachusetts Institute of Technology.
Description: Cambridge, United Kingdom ; New York, NY, USA : Cambridge
University Press, 2018. | Includes bibliographical references.
Identifiers: LCCN 2018005020 | ISBN 9781107184589 (hardback) |
ISBN 9781316636008 (paperback)
Subjects: LCSH: Machine learning–Mathematics. | Computer algorithms.
Classification: LCC Q325.5 .M65 2018 | DDC 006.3/1015181–dc23
LC record available at https://lccn.loc.gov/2018005020

ISBN 978-1-107-18458-9 Hardback
ISBN 978-1-316-63600-8 Paperback

Contents

Preface

The monograph is based on the class Algorithmic Aspects of Machine Learning taught at MIT in fall 2013, spring 2015, and fall 2017. Thank you to all the students and postdocs who participated in this class and made teaching it a wonderful experience.

1

Introduction

Machine learning is starting to take over decision-making in many aspects of our life, including:

(a) keeping us safe on our daily commute in self-driving cars,
(b) making accurate diagnoses based on our symptoms and medical history,
(c) pricing and trading complex securities, and
(d) discovering new science, such as the genetic basis for various diseases.

But the startling truth is that these algorithms work without any sort of provable guarantees on their behavior. When they are faced with an optimization problem, do they actually find the best solution, or even a pretty good one? When they posit a probabilistic model, can they incorporate new evidence and sample from the true posterior distribution? Machine learning works amazingly well in practice, but that doesn't mean we understand *why* it works so well.

If you've taken traditional algorithms courses, the usual way you've been exposed to thinking about algorithms is through worst-case analysis. When you have a sorting algorithm, you measure its running time based on how many operations it takes on the worst possible input. That's a convenient type of bound to have, because it means you can say meaningful things about how long your algorithm takes without ever worrying about the types of inputs you usually give it.

But what makes analyzing machine learning algorithms, especially modern ones, so challenging is that the types of problems they are trying to solve really are *NP*-hard on worst-case inputs. When you cast the problem of finding the parameters that best fit your data as an optimization problem, there are instances where it is *NP*-hard to find a good fit. When you posit a probabilistic model and want to use it to perform inference, there are instances where that is *NP*-hard as well.

1

In this book, we will approach the problem of giving provable guarantees for machine learning by trying to find more realistic models for our data. In many applications, there are reasonable assumptions we can make, based on the context in which the problem came up, that can get us around these worst-case impediments and allow us to rigorously analyze heuristics that are used in practice, as well as design fundamentally new ways of solving some of the central, recurring problems in machine learning.

To take a step back, the idea of moving beyond worst-case analysis is an idea that is as old[1] as theoretical computer science itself [95]. In fact, there are many different flavors of what it means to understand the behavior of algorithms on "typical" instances, including:

(a) probabilistic models for your input, or even hybrid models that combine elements of worst-case and average-case analysis like semi-random models [38, 71] or smoothed analysis [39, 130];

(b) ways to measure the complexity of your problem and ask for algorithms that are fast on simple inputs, as in parameterized complexity [66]; and

(c) notions of stability that attempt to articulate what instances of your problem have meaningful answers and are the ones you actually want to solve [20, 32].

This is by no means an exhaustive list of topics or references. Regardless, in this book, we will approach machine learning problems armed with these sorts of insights about ways to get around intractability.

Ultimately, we hope that theoretical computer science and machine learning have a lot left to teach each other. Understanding why heuristics like expectation- maximization or gradient descent on a nonconvex function work so well in practice is a grand challenge for theoretical computer science. But to make progress on these questions, we need to understand what types of models and assumptions make sense in the context of machine learning. On the other hand, if we make progress on these hard problems and develop new insights about *why* heuristics work so well, we can hope to engineer them better. We can even hope to discover totally new ways to solve some of the important problems in machine learning, especially by leveraging modern tools in our algorithmic toolkit.

In this book, we will cover the following topics:

(a) Nonnegative matrix factorization

(b) Topic modeling

---

[1] After all, heuristics performing well on real life inputs are old as well (long predating modern machine learning), hence so is the need to explain them.

(c) Tensor decompositions
(d) Sparse recovery
(e) Sparse coding
(f) Learning mixtures models
(g) Matrix completion

I hope more chapters will be added in later versions as the field develops and makes new discoveries.

2

Nonnegative Matrix Factorization

In this chapter, we will explore the nonnegative matrix factorization problem. It will be helpful to first compare it to the more familiar singular value decomposition. In the worst case, the nonnegative matrix factorization problem is *NP*-hard (seriously, what else did you expect?), but we will make domain-specific assumptions (called *separability*) that will allow us to give provable algorithms for an important special case of it. We then apply our algorithms to the problem of learning the parameters of a topic model. This will be our first case study in how to not back down in the face of computational intractability, and to find ways around it.

2.1 Introduction

In order to better understand the motivations behind the nonnegative matrix factorization problem and why it is useful in applications, it will be helpful to first introduce the singular value decomposition and then compare the two. Eventually, we will apply both of these to text analysis later in this section.

The Singular Value Decomposition

The singular value decomposition (SVD) is one of the most useful tools in linear algebra. Given an $m \times n$ matrix M, its singular value decomposition is written as

$$M = U\Sigma V^T$$

where U and V are orthonormal and Σ is a rectangular matrix with nonzero entries only along the diagonal, and its entries are nonnegative. Alternatively, we can write

4

$$M = \sum_{i=1}^{r} \sigma_i u_i v_i^T$$

where u_i is the ith column of U, v_i is the ith column of V, and σ_i is the ith diagonal entry of Σ. Throughout this section we will fix the convention that $\sigma_1 \geq \sigma_2 \geq \ldots \geq \sigma_r > 0$. In this case, the rank of M is precisely r.

Throughout this book, we will have occasion to use this decomposition as well as the (perhaps more familiar) eigendecomposition. If M is an $n \times n$ matrix and is diagonalizable, its eigendecomposition is written as

$$M = PDP^{-1}$$

where D is diagonal. For now, the important facts to remember are:

(1) **Existence:** Every matrix has a singular value decomposition, even if it is rectangular. In contrast, a matrix must be square to have an eigendecomposition. Even then, not all square matrices can be diagonalized, but a sufficient condition under which M can be diagonalized is that all its eigenvalues are distinct.
(2) **Algorithms:** Both of these decompositions can be computed efficiently. The best general algorithms for computing the singular value decomposition run in time $O(mn^2)$ if $m \geq n$. There are also faster algorithms for sparse matrices. There are algorithms to compute an eigendecomposition in $O(n^3)$ time and there are further improvements based on fast matrix multiplication, although it is not clear whether such algorithms are as stable and practical.
(3) **Uniqueness:** The singular value decomposition is unique if and only if its singular values are distinct. Similarly, the eigendecomposition is unique if and only if its eigenvalues are distinct. In some cases, we will only need that the nonzero singular values/eigenvalues are distinct, because we can ignore the others.

Two Applications

Two of the most important properties of the singular value decomposition are that it can be used to find the best rank k approximation and that it can be used for dimension reduction. We explore these next. First, let's formalize what we mean by the best rank k approximation problem. One way to do this is to work with the Frobenius norm:

Definition 2.1.1 (Frobenius norm) $\|M\|_F = \sqrt{\sum_{i,j} M_{i,j}^2}$

It is easy to see that the Frobenius norm is invariant under rotations. For example, this follows by considering each of the columns of M separately as a vector. The square of the Frobenius norm of a matrix is the sum of squares of the norms of its columns. Then left-multiplying by an orthogonal matrix preserves the norm of each of its columns. An identical argument holds for right-multiplying by an orthogonal matrix (but working with the rows instead). This invariance allows us to give an alternative characterization of the Frobenius norm that is quite useful:

$$\|M\|_F = \|U^T M V\|_F = \|\Sigma\|_F = \sqrt{\sum \sigma_i^2}$$

The first equality is where all the action is happening and uses the rotational invariance property we established above.

Then the Eckart–Young theorem asserts that the best rank k approximation to some matrix M (in terms of Frobenius norm) is given by its truncated singular value decomposition:

Theorem 2.1.2 (Eckart–Young) $\operatorname*{argmin}_{\mathrm{rank}(B)\leq k} \|M - B\|_F = \sum_{i=1}^{k} \sigma_i u_i v_i^T$

Let M_k be the best rank k approximation. Then, from our alternative definition of the Frobenius norm, it is immediate that $\|M - M_k\|_F = \sqrt{\sum_{i=k+1}^{r} \sigma_i^2}$.

In fact, the same statement – that the best rank k approximation to M is its truncated singular value decomposition – holds for *any* norm that is invariant under rotations. As another application, consider the operator norm:

Definition 2.1.3 (operator norm) $\|M\| = \max_{\|x\|\leq 1} \|Mx\|$

It is easy to see that the operator norm is also invariant under rotations and, moreover, $\|M\| = \sigma_1$, again using the convention that σ_1 is the largest singular value. Then the Eckart–Young theorem with respect to the operator norm asserts:

Theorem 2.1.4 (Eckart–Young) $\operatorname*{argmin}_{\mathrm{rank}(B)\leq k} \|M - B\| = \sum_{i=1}^{k} \sigma_i u_i v_i^T$

Again, let M_k be the best rank k approximation. Then $\|M - M_k\| = \sigma_{k+1}$. As a quick check, if $k \geq r$ then $\sigma_{k+1} = 0$, and the best rank k approximation is exact and has no error (as it should). You should think of this as something you can do with any algorithm to compute the singular value decomposition of M – you can find the best rank k approximation to it with respect to any rotationally invariant norm. In fact, it is remarkable that the best rank k approximation in many different norms coincides! Moreover, the best rank k approximation to

M can be obtained directly from its best rank $k + 1$ approximation. This is not always the case, as we will see in the next chapter when we work with tensors.

Next, we give an entirely different application of the singular value decomposition in the context of data analysis before we move on to applications of it in text analysis. Recall that M is an $m \times n$ matrix. We can think of it as defining a distribution on n-dimensional vectors, which we obtain from choosing one of its columns uniformly at random. Further suppose that $\mathbb{E}[x] = 0$; i.e., the columns sum to the all-zero vector. Let $\mathcal{P}_k$ be the space of all projections onto a k-dimensional subspace.

Theorem 2.1.5 $\underset{P \in \mathcal{P}_k}{\mathrm{argmax}}\ \mathbb{E}[\|Px\|^2] = \sum_{i=1}^{k} u_i u_i^T$

This is another basic theorem about the singular value decomposition, and from it we can readily compute the k-dimensional projection that maximizes the projected variance. This theorem is often invoked in visualization, where one can visualize high-dimensional vector data by projecting it to a more manageable lower-dimensional subspace.

Latent Semantic Indexing

Now that we have developed some of the intuition behind the singular value decomposition, we will see an application of it to text analysis. One of the central problems in this area (and one that we will return to many times) is this: given a large collection of documents, we want to extract some hidden *thematic* structure. Deerwester et al. [60] invented latent semantic indexing (LSI) for this purpose, and their approach was to apply the singular value decomposition to what is usually called the term-by-document matrix:

Definition 2.1.6 *The term-by-document matrix M is an $m \times n$ matrix where each row represents a word and each column represents a document where*

$$M_{i,j} = \frac{\text{count of word } i \text{ in document } j}{\text{total number of words in document } j}.$$

There are many popular normalization conventions, and here we have chosen to normalize the matrix so that each of its columns sums to one. In this way, we can interpret each document as a probability distribution on words. Also, in constructing the term-by-document matrix, we have ignored the order in which the words occur. This is called a *bag-of-words representation*, and the justification for it comes from a thought experiment. Suppose I were to give you the words contained in a document, but in a jumbled order. It should still be possible to determine what the document is about, and hence forgetting all notions of syntax and grammar and representing a document as a vector loses some structure, but should preserve enough of the information to make many basic tasks in text analysis still possible.

Once our data is in vector form, we can make use of tools from linear algebra. How can we measure the similarities between two documents? The naive approach is to base our similarity measure on how many words they have in common. Let's try

$$\langle M_i, M_j \rangle.$$

This quantity computes the probability that a randomly chosen word w from document i and a randomly chosen word w' from document j are the same. But what makes this a bad measure is that when documents are sparse, they may not have many words in common just by accident because of the particular words each author chose to use to describe the same types of things. Even worse, some documents could be deemed to be similar because they contain many of the same common words, which have little to do with what the documents are actually about.

Deerwester et al. [60] proposed to use the singular value decomposition of M to compute a more reasonable measure of similarity, and one that seems to work better when the term-by-document matrix is sparse (as it usually is). Let $M = U\Sigma V^T$ and let $U_{1...k}$ and $V_{1...k}$ be the first k columns of U and V, respectively. The approach is to compute

$$\langle U_{1...k}^T M_i, U_{1...k}^T M_j \rangle$$

for each pair of documents. The intuition is that there are some *topics* that occur over and over again in the collection of documents. And if we could represent each document M_i on the basis of topics, then their inner product on that basis would yield a more meaningful measure of similarity. There are some models – i.e., hypotheses for how the data is stochastically generated – where it can be shown that this approach provably recovers the true topics [118]. This is the ideal interaction between theory and practice – we have techniques that work (somewhat) well, and we can analyze/justify them.

However, there are many failings of latent semantic indexing that have motivated alternative approaches. If we associate the top singular vectors with topics, then

(1) topics are orthonormal.

However, topics like *politics* and *finance* actually contain many words in common, so they cannot be orthonormal.

(2) topics contain negative values.

Hence, if a document contains such words, their contribution (to the topic) could cancel out the contributions from other words. Moreover, a pair of documents can be judged to be similar because of particular topics that they are both not about.

Nonnegative Matrix Factorization

For exactly the failings we described in the previous section, nonnegative matrix factorization is a popular alternative to the singular value decomposition in many applications in text analysis. However, it has its own shortcomings. Unlike the singular value decomposition, it is *NP*-hard to compute. And the prevailing approach in practice is to rely on heuristics, with no provable guarantees.

Definition 2.1.7 *A nonnegative matrix factorization of inner-dimension r is a decomposition*

$$M = AW$$

where A is n × r, W is r × n, and both are entrywise nonnegative. Moreover, let the nonnegative rank of M – denoted by $\text{rank}^+(M)$ *– be the minimum r so that such a factorization exists.*

As we will see, this factorization, when applied to a term-by-document matrix, can find more interpretable topics. Beyond text analysis, it has many other applications in machine learning and statistics, including in collaborative filtering and image segmentation. For now, let's give an interpretation of a nonnegative matrix factorization specifically in the context of text analysis. Suppose we apply it to a term-by-document matrix. Then it turns out that we can always put it in a convenient canonical form: Let D be a diagonal matrix where

$$D_{j,j} = \sum_{i=1}^{m} A_{i,j}$$

and further suppose that each $D_{j,j} > 0$. Then

Claim 2.1.8 *Set* $\widetilde{A} = AD^{-1}$ *and* $\widetilde{W} = DW$. *Then*

(1) $\widetilde{A}, \widetilde{W}$ *are entrywise nonnegative and* $M = \widetilde{A}\widetilde{W}$, *and*
(2) the columns of $\widetilde{A}$ *and the columns of* $\widetilde{W}$ *each sum to one.*

We leave the proof of this claim as an exercise, but the hint is that property (2) follows because the columns of M also sum to one.

Hence we can, without loss of generality, assume that our nonnegative matrix factorization $M = AW$ is such that the columns of A and the columns of W each sum to one. Then we can interpret this factorization as follows: Each document is itself a distribution on words, and what we have found is

(1) a collection of r topics – the columns of A – that are themselves distributions on words, and
(2) for each document i, a representation of it – given by W_i – as a convex combination of r topics so that we recover its original distribution on words.

Later on, we will get some insight into why nonnegative matrix factorization is NP-hard. But what approaches are used in practice to actually compute such a factorization? The usual approach is *alternating minimization*:

Alternating Minimization for NMF

Input: $M \in \mathbb{R}^{m \times n}$
Output: $M \approx A^{(N)} W^{(N)}$

Guess entrywise nonnegative $A^{(0)}$ of dimension $m \times r$
For $i = 1$ to N
    Set $W^{(i)} \leftarrow \mathrm{argmin}_W \|M - A^{(i-1)} W\|_F^2$ s.t. $W \geq 0$
    Set $A^{(i)} \leftarrow \mathrm{argmin}_A \|M - AW^{(i)}\|_F^2$ s.t. $A \geq 0$
End

Alternating minimization is quite general, and throughout this book we will come back to it many times and find that problems we are interested in are solved in practice using some variant of the basic approach above. However, it has no provable guarantees in the traditional sense. It can fail by getting stuck in a locally optimal solution that is much worse than the globally optimal one. In fact, this is inevitable, because the problem it is attempting to solve really is NP-hard.

However, in many settings we will be able to make progress by working with an appropriate stochastic model, where we will be able to show that it converges to a globally optimal solution provably. A major theme in this book is to not take for granted heuristics that seem to work in practice "as immutable," because the ability to analyze them will itself provide new insights into when and why they work, and also what can go wrong and how to improve them.

2.2 Algebraic Algorithms

In the previous section, we introduced the nonnegative matrix factorization problem and described some of its applications in machine learning and statistics. In fact, because of the algebraic nature of the problem, it is far from clear that there is any finite time algorithm for computing it in the worst case. Here we will explore some of the fundamental results in solving systems of polynomial equations, and derive algorithms for nonnegative matrix factorization from these.

Rank vs. Nonnegative Rank

Recall that $\text{rank}^+(M)$ is the smallest value r such that M has a nonnegative matrix factorization $M = AW$ with inner dimension r. It is easy to see that the following is an equivalent definition:

Claim 2.2.1 *$\text{rank}^+(M)$ is the smallest r such that there are r entrywise nonnegative rank one matrices $\{M_i\}$ that satisfy $M = \sum_i M_i$.*

We can now compare the rank and the nonnegative rank. There are, of course, many equivalent definitions for the rank of a matrix, but the most convenient definition to compare the two is the following:

Claim 2.2.2 *$\text{rank}(M)$ is the smallest r such that there are r rank one matrices $\{M_i\}$ that satisfy $M = \sum_i M_i$.*

The only difference between these two definitions is that the former stipulates that all of the rank one matrices in the decomposition are entrywise nonnegative, while the latter does not. Thus it follows immediately that

Fact 2.2.3 *$\text{rank}^+(M) \geq \text{rank}(M)$*

Can the nonnegative rank of a matrix be much larger than its rank? We encourage the reader to think about this question before proceeding. This is equivalent to asking whether, for an entrywise nonnegative matrix M, one can, without loss of generality, require the factors in its rank decomposition to be entrywise nonnegative too. It is certainly true for a rank one matrix, and turns out to be true for a rank two matrix too, but...

In general, the nonnegative rank cannot be bounded by any function of the rank alone. In fact, the relationship (or lack thereof) between the rank and the nonnegative rank is of fundamental importance in a number of areas in theoretical computer science. Fortunately, there are simple examples that illustrate that the two parameters can be far apart:

Example: Let M be an $n \times n$ matrix where $M_{ij} = (i - j)^2$.

It is easy to see that the column space of M is spanned by the following three vectors:

$$\begin{bmatrix} 1 \\ 1 \\ \vdots \\ 1 \end{bmatrix}, \begin{bmatrix} 1 \\ 2 \\ \vdots \\ n \end{bmatrix}, \begin{bmatrix} 1 \\ 4 \\ \vdots \\ n^2 \end{bmatrix}.$$

Hence $\text{rank}(M) \leq 3$. (In fact, $\text{rank}(M) = 3$.) However, M has zeros along the diagonal and nonzeros off the diagonal. Furthermore, for any rank one entrywise nonnegative matrix M_i, its pattern of zeros and nonzeros is a *combinatorial rectangle* – i.e., the intersection of some set of rows and columns – and it can be shown that one needs at least $\log n$ such rectangles to cover the nonzeros of M without covering any of its zeros. Hence:

Fact 2.2.4 $\text{rank}^+(M) \geq \log n$

A word of caution: For this example, a number of authors have incorrectly tried to prove a much stronger lower bound (e.g., $\text{rank}^+(M) = n$). In fact (and somewhat surprisingly), it turns out that $\text{rank}^+(M) \leq 2 \log n$. The usual error is in thinking that because the rank of a matrix is the largest r such that it has r linearly independent columns, the nonnegative rank is the largest r such that there are r columns where no column is a convex combination of the other $r - 1$. This is not true!

Systems of Polynomial Inequalities

We can reformulate the problem of deciding whether $\text{rank}^+(M) \leq r$ is a problem of finding a feasible solution to a particular system of polynomial inequalities. More specifically, $\text{rank}^+(M) \leq r$ if and only if

$$\begin{cases} M = AW \\ A \geq 0 \\ W \geq 0 \end{cases} \tag{2.1}$$

has a solution. This system consists of quadratic equality constraints (one for each entry of M) and linear inequalities that require A and W to be entrywise nonnegative. Before we worry about fast algorithms, we should ask a more basic question (whose answer is not at all obvious):

Question 4 *Is there any finite time algorithm for deciding if* $\text{rank}^+(M) \leq r$?

This is equivalent to deciding if the above linear system has a solution, but the difficulty is that even if there is one, the entries of A and W could be irrational. This is quite different than, say, 3-SAT, where there is a simple brute-force algorithm. In contrast, for nonnegative matrix factorization it is quite challenging to design algorithms that run in any finite amount of time.

But indeed there are algorithms (that run in some fixed amount of time) to decide whether a system of polynomial inequalities has a solution or not in the real RAM model. The first finite time algorithm for solving a system of polynomial inequalities follows from the seminal work of Tarski, and there has been a long line of improvements based on successively more powerful algebraic decompositions. This line of work culminated in the following algorithm of Renegar:

Theorem 2.2.5 *[126] Given a system of m polynomial inequalities in k variables, whose maximum degree is D and whose bit complexity is L, there is an algorithm whose running time is*

$$(nDL)^{O(k)}$$

that decides whether the system has a solution. Moreover, if it does have a solution, then it outputs a polynomial and an interval (one for each variable) in which there is only one root, which is the value of the variable in the true solution.

Notice that this algorithm finds an implicit representation of the solution, since you can find as many bits of the solution as you would like by performing a binary search for the root. Moreover, this algorithm is essentially optimal, and improving it would yield subexponential time algorithms for 3-SAT.

We can use these algorithms to solve nonnegative matrix factorization, and it immediately implies that there is an algorithm for deciding if $\text{rank}^+(M) \leq r$ runs in exponential time. However, the number of variables we would need in the naive representation is $nr + mr$, one for each entry in A or W. So even if $r = O(1)$, we would need a linear number of variables and the running time would still be exponential. It turns that even though the naive representation uses many variables, there is a more clever representation that uses many fewer variables.

Variable Reduction

Here we explore the idea of finding a system of polynomial equations that expresses the nonnegative matrix factorization problem using many fewer variables. In [13, 112], Arora et al. and Moitra gave a system of polynomial inequalities with $f(r) = 2r^2$ variables that has a solution if and only if $\text{rank}^+(M) \leq r$. This immediately yields a polynomial time algorithm to compute a nonnegative matrix factorization of inner-dimension r (if it exists) for any $r = O(1)$. These algorithms turn out to be essentially optimal in a worst-case sense, and prior to this work the best known algorithms even for the case $r = 4$ ran in exponential time.

We will focus on a special case to illustrate the basic idea behind variable reduction. Suppose that $\text{rank}(M) = r$, and our goal is to decide whether or not $\text{rank}^+(M) = r$. This is called the simplicial factorization problem. Can we find an alternate system of polynomial inequalities that expresses this decision problem but uses many fewer variables? The following simple but useful observation will pave the way:

Claim 2.2.6 *In any solution to the simplicial factorization problem, A and W must have full column and row rank, respectively.*

Proof: If $M = AW$, then the column span of A must contain the columns of M, and similarly, the row span of W must contain the rows of M. Since $\text{rank}(M) = r$, we conclude that A and W must have r linearly independent columns and rows, respectively. Since A has r columns and W has r rows, this implies the claim. ∎

Hence we know that A has a left pseudo-inverse A^+ and W has a right pseudo-inverse W^+ so that $A^+A = WW^+I_r$, where I_r is the $r \times r$ identity matrix. We will make use of these pseudo-inverses to reduce the number of variables in our system of polynomial inequalities. In particular:

$$A^+AW = W$$

so we can recover the columns of W from a linear transformation of the columns of M. Similarly, we can recover the rows of A from a linear transformation of the rows of M. This leads to the following alternative system of polynomial inequalities:

$$\begin{cases} MW^+A^+M = M \\ MW^+ \qquad\ \geq 0 \\ A^+M \qquad\ \ \geq 0 \end{cases} \tag{2.2}$$

A priori, it is not clear that we have made progress, since this system also has $nr + mr$ variables corresponding to the entries of A^+ and W^+. However, consider the matrix MW^+. If we represent S^+ as an $n \times r$ matrix, then we are describing its action on all vectors, but the crucial observation is that we only need to know how S^+ acts on the rows of M that span an r-dimensional space. Hence we can apply a change of basis to write

$$M_C = MU$$

where U is an $n \times r$ matrix that has a right pseudo-inverse. Similarly, we can write

$$M_R = VM$$

where V is an $r \times m$ matrix that has a left pseudo-inverse. Now we get a new system:

$$\begin{cases} M_C S T M_R = M \\ M_C S \quad \geq 0 \\ T M_R \quad \geq 0 \end{cases} \tag{2.3}$$

Notice that S and T are both $r \times r$ matrices, and hence there are $2r^2$ variables in total. Moreover, this formulation is equivalent to the simplicial factorization problem in the following sense:

Claim 2.2.7 *If* $rank(M) = rank^+(M) = r$, *then (2.3) has a solution.*

Proof: Using the notation above, we can set $S = U^+ W^+$ and $T = A^+ V^+$. Then $M_C S = M U U^+ W^+ = A$ and similarly $T M_R = A^+ V^+ V M = W$, and this implies the claim. ∎

This is often called *completeness*, since if there is a solution to the original problem, we want there to be a valid solution to our reformulation. We also need to prove *soundness*, that any solution to the reformulation yields a valid solution to the original problem:

Claim 2.2.8 *If there is a solution to (2.3), then there is a solution to (2.1).*

Proof: For any solution to (2.3), we can set $A = M_C S$ and $W = T M_R$, and it follows that $A, W \geq 0$ and $M = AW$. ∎

It turns out to be quite involved to extend the ideas above to nonnegative matrix factorization in general. The main idea in [112] is to first establish a new normal form for nonnegative matrix factorization, and use the observation that even though A could have exponentially many maximal sets of linearly independent columns, their psueudo-inverses are algebraically dependent and can be expressed over a common set of r^2 variables using Cramer's rule. Additionally, Arora et al. [13] showed that any algorithm that solves even the simplicial factorization problem in $(nm)^{o(r)}$ time yields a subexponential time algorithm for 3-SAT, and hence the algorithms above are nearly optimal under standard complexity assumptions.

Further Remarks

Earlier in this section, we gave a simple example that illustrates a separation between the rank and the nonnegative rank. In fact, there are more interesting examples of separations that come up in theoretical computer science, where a natural question is to express a particular polytope P in n dimensions, which has exponentially many facets as the projection of a higher dimensional polytope Q with only polynomially many facets. This is called an *extended formulation*, and a deep result of Yannakakis is that the minimum number of facets of any such Q – called the *extension complexity* of P – is precisely equal to the nonnegative rank of some matrix that has to do with the geometric arrangement between vertices and facets of P [144]. Then the fact that there are explicit polytopes P whose extension complexity is exponential is intimately related to finding explicit matrices that exhibit large separations between their rank and nonnegative rank.

Furthermore, the nonnegative rank also has important applications in communication complexity, where one of the most important open questions – the *log-rank conjecture* [108] – can be reformulated by asking: Given a Boolean matrix M, is $\log \operatorname{rank}^+(M) \leq (\log \operatorname{rank}(M))^{O(1)}$? Thus, in the example above, the fact that the nonnegative rank cannot be bounded by any function of the rank could be due to the entries of M taking on many distinct values.

2.3 Stability and Separability

Here we will give a geometric (as opposed to algebraic) interpretation of nonnegative matrix factorization that will offer new insights into why it is hard in the worst case and what types of features make it easy. In particular, we will move beyond worst-case analysis and work with a new assumption called *separability* that will allow us to give an algorithm that runs in polynomial time (even for large values of r). This assumption was first introduced to understand conditions under which the nonnegative matrix factorization problem has a unique solution [65], and this is a common theme in algorithm design

Theme 1 *Looking for cases where the solution is unique and robust will often point to cases where we can design algorithms with provable guarantees in spite of worst-case hardness results.*

Cones and Intermediate Simplicies

Here we will develop some geometric intuition about nonnegative matrix factorization – or, rather, an important special case of it called simplicial factorization that we introduced in the previous section. First, let us introduce the notion of a cone:

Definition 2.3.1 *Let A be an $m \times r$ matrix. Then the cone generated by the columns of A is*

$$\mathcal{C}_A = \{Ax | x \geq 0\}.$$

We can immediately connect this to nonnegative matrix factorization.

Claim 2.3.2 *Given matrix M, A of dimension $m \times n$ and $m \times r$, respectively, there is an entrywise nonnegative matrix W of dimension $r \times n$ with $M = AW$ if and only if $\mathcal{C}_M \subseteq \mathcal{C}_A$.*

Proof: In the forward direction, suppose $M = AW$, where W is entrywise nonnegative. Then any vector $y \in \mathcal{C}_M$ can be written as $y = Mx$ where $x \geq 0$, and then $y = AWx$ and the vector $Wx \geq 0$, and hence $y \in \mathcal{C}_A$ too. In the reverse direction, suppose $\mathcal{C}_M \subseteq \mathcal{C}_A$. Then any column $M_i \in \mathcal{C}_A$ and we can write $M_i = AW_i$ where $W_i \geq 0$. Now we can set W to be the matrix whose columns are $\{W_i\}_i$ and this completes the proof. ∎

What makes nonnegative matrix factorization difficult is that both A and W are unknown (if one were known, say A, then we could solve for the other by setting up an appropriate linear program, which amounts to representing each column of M in $\mathcal{C}_A$).

Vavasis [139] was the first to introduce the simplicial factorization problem, and one of his motivations was that it turns out to be connected to a purely geometric problem about fitting a simplex in between two given polytopes. This is called the intermediate simplex problem:

Definition 2.3.3 *An instance of the intermediate simplex problem consists of P and Q with $P \subseteq Q \subseteq \mathbb{R}^{r-1}$, and P is specified by its vertices and Q is specified by its facets. The goal is to find a simplex K with $P \subseteq K \subseteq Q$.*

In the next section we will show that the simplicial factorization problem and the intermediate simplex problem are equivalent.

Reductions

We will prove that the simplicial factorization problem and the intermediate simplex problem are equivalent in the sense that there is a polynomial time reduction in both directions. We will do so by way of a few intermediate problems.

Suppose we are given an instance of the simplicial factorization problem. Then we can write $M = UV$, where U and V have inner dimension r but are not necessarily entrywise nonnegative. If we can find an invertible $r \times r$ matrix T where UT and $T^{-1}V$ are both entrywise nonnegative, then we have found a valid nonnegative matrix factorization with inner dimension r.

Claim 2.3.4 *If rank$(M) = r$ and $M = UV$ and $M = AW$ are two factorizations that have inner-dimension r, then*

(1) colspan$(U) = $ colspan$(A) = $ colspan(M) and
(2) rowspan$(V) = $ rowspan$(W) = $ rowspan(M).

This follows from basic facts in linear algebra, and implies that any two such factorizations $M = UV$ and $M = AW$ can be linearly transformed into each other via some invertible $r \times r$ matrix T. Hence the intermediate simplex problem is equivalent to

Definition 2.3.5 *An instance of the problem **P1** consists of an $m \times n$ entrywise nonnegative matrix M with rank$(M) = r$ and $M = UV$ with inner dimension r. The goal is to find an invertible $r \times r$ matrix where both UT and $T^{-1}V$ are entrywise nonnegative.*

Caution: The fact that you can start out with an arbitrary factorization and ask to rotate it into a nonnegative matrix factorization of minimum inner dimension but haven't painted yourself into a corner is particular to the simplicial factorization problem only! It is generally not true when rank$(M) <$ rank$^+(M)$.

Now we can give a geometric interoperation of **P1**:

(1) Let $u_1, u_2, \ldots, u_m$ be the rows of U.
(2) Let $t_1, t_2, \ldots, t_r$ be the columns of T.
(3) Let $v_1, v_2, \ldots, v_n$ be the columns of V.

We will first work with an intermediate cone problem, but its connection to the intermediate simplex problem will be immediate. Toward that end, let P be the cone generated by $u_1, u_2, \ldots, u_m$, and let K be the cone generated by $t_1, t_2, \ldots, t_r$. Finally, let Q be the cone given by

$$Q = \{x | \langle u_i, x \rangle \geq 0 \text{ for all } i\}.$$

It is not hard to see that Q is a cone in the sense that it is generated as all nonnegative combinations of a finite set of vectors (its extreme rays), but we have instead chosen to represent it by its supporting hyperplanes (through the origin).

Claim 2.3.6 *UT is entrywise nonnegative if and only if $\{t_1, t_2, \ldots, t_r\} \subseteq Q$.*

This follows immediately from the definition of Q, because the rows of U are its supporting hyperplanes (through the origin). Hence we have a geometric reformulation of the constraint UT that is entrywise nonnegative in **P1**. Next, we will interpret the other constraint, that $T^{-1}V$ is entrywise nonnegative too.

Claim 2.3.7 *$T^{-1}V$ is entrywise nonnegative if and only if $\{v_1, v_2, \ldots, v_m\} \subseteq K$.*

Proof: Consider $x_i = T^{-1}v_i$. Then $Tx_i = T(T^{-1})v_i = v_i$, and hence x_i is a representation of v_i as a linear combination of $\{t_1, t_2, \ldots, t_r\}$. Moreover, it is the unique representation, and this completes the proof. ∎

Thus **P1** is equivalent to the following problem:

Definition 2.3.8 *An instance of the intermediate cone problem consists of cones P and Q with $P \subseteq Q \subseteq \mathbb{R}^{r-1}$, and P is specified by its extreme rays and Q is specified by its supporting hyperplanes (through the origin). The goal is to find a cone K with r extreme rays and $P \subseteq K \subseteq Q$.*

Furthermore, the intermediate cone problem is easily seen to be equivalent to the intermediate simplex problem by intersecting the cones in it with a hyperplane, in which case a cone with extreme rays becomes a convex hull of the intersection of those rays with the hyperplane.

Geometric Gadgets

Vavasis made use of the equivalences in the previous section to construct certain geometric gadgets to prove that nonnegative matrix factorization is *NP*-hard. The idea was to construct a two-dimensional gadget where there are only two possible intermediate triangles, which can then be used to represent the truth assignment for a variable x_i. The description of the complete reduction and the proof of its soundness are involved (see [139]).

Theorem 2.3.9 *[139] Nonnegative matrix factorization, simplicial factorization, intermediate simplex, intermediate cone, and **P1** are all NP-hard.*

Arora et al. [13] improved upon this reduction by constructing low-dimensional gadgets with many more choices. This allows them to reduce from the d-SUM problem, where we are given a set of n numbers and the goal is to find a set of d of them that sum to zero. The best known algorithms for this problem run in time roughly $n^{\lceil d/2 \rceil}$. Again, the full construction and the proof of soundness are involved.

Theorem 2.3.10 *Nonnegative matrix factorization, simplicial factorization, intermediate simplex, intermediate cone, and* **P1** *all require time at least* $(nm)^{\Omega(r)}$ *unless there is a subexponential time algorithm for 3-SAT.*

In all of the topics we will cover, it is important to understand what makes the problem hard in order to identify what makes it easy. The common feature in all of the above gadgets is that the gadgets themselves are highly unstable and have multiple solutions, and so it is natural to look for instances where the answer itself is robust and unique in order to identify instances that can be solved more efficiently than in the worst case.

Separability

In fact, Donoho and Stodden [64] were among the first to explore the question of what sorts of conditions imply that the nonnegative matrix factorization of minimum inner dimension is unique. Their original examples came from toy problems in image segmentation, but it seems like the condition itself can most naturally be interpreted in the setting of text analysis.

Definition 2.3.11 *We call A separable if, for every column i of A, there is a row j where the only nonzero is in the ith column. Furthermore, we call j an anchor word for column i.*

In fact, separability is quite natural in the context of text analysis. Recall that we interpret the columns of A as topics. We can think of separability as the promise that these topics come with *anchor words*; informally, for each topic there is an unknown anchor word, and if it occurs in a document, the document is (partially) about the given topic. For example, *401k* could be an anchor word for the topic *personal finance*. It seems that natural language contains many such highly specific words.

We will now give an algorithm for finding the anchor words and for solving instances of nonnegative matrix factorization where the unknown A is separable in polynomial time.

Theorem 2.3.12 *[13] If M = AW and A is separable and W has full row rank, then the* **Anchor Words Algorithm** *outputs A and W (up to rescaling).*

Why do anchor words help? It is easy to see that if A is separable, then the rows of W appear as rows of M (after scaling). Hence we just need to determine which rows of M correspond to anchor words. We know from our discussion in Section 2.3 that if we scale M, A, and W so that their rows sum to one, the convex hull of the rows of W contains the rows of M. But since these rows appear in M as well, we can try to find W by iteratively deleting rows of M that do not change its convex hull.

Let M^i denote the ith row of M and let M^I denote the restriction of M to the rows in I for $I \subseteq [n]$. So now we can find the anchor words using the following simple procedure:

Find Anchors [13]

Input: matrix $M \in \mathbb{R}^{m \times n}$ satisfying the conditions in Theorem 2.3.12
Output: $W = M^I$

Delete duplicate rows:
Set $I = [n]$
For $i = 1, 2, \ldots, n$
    If $M^i \in \text{conv}(\{M^j | j \in I, j \neq i\})$, set $I \leftarrow I - \{i\}$
End

Here in the first step, we want to remove redundant rows. If two rows are scalar multiples of each other, then one being in the cone generated by the rows of W implies the other is too, so we can safely delete one of the two rows. We do this for all rows, so that in the equivalence class of rows that are scalar multiples of each other, exactly one remains. We will not focus on this technicality in our discussion, though.

It is easy to see that deleting a row of M that is not an anchor word will not change the convex hull of the remaining rows, and so the above algorithm terminates with a set I that only contains anchor words. Moreover, at termination

$$\text{conv}(\{M^i | i \in I\}) = \text{conv}(\{M^j\}_j).$$

Alternatively, the convex hull is the same as at the start. Hence the anchor words that are deleted are redundant and we can just as well do without them.

Anchor Words [13]

Input: matrix $M \in \mathbb{R}^{n \times m}$ satisfying the conditions in Theorem 2.3.12
Output: A, W

Run **Find Anchors** on M, let W be the output
Solve for nonnegative A that minimizes $\|M - AW\|_F$ (convex programming)
End

The proof of theorem follows immediately from the proof of correctness of **Find Anchors** and the fact that $\text{conv}(\{M^i\}_i) \subseteq \text{conv}(\{W^i\}_i)$ if and only if there is a nonnegative A (whose rows sum to one) with $M = AW$.

The above algorithm, when naively implemented, would be prohibitively slow. Instead, there have been many improvements to the algorithm ([33], [100], [78]), and we will describe one in particular that appears in [12]. Suppose we choose a row M^i at random. Then it is easy to see that the farthest row from M^i will be an anchor word.

Similarly, if we have found one anchor word, the farthest row from it will be another anchor word, and so on. In this way we can greedily find all of the anchor rows, and moreover, this method only relies on pairwise distances and projection, so we can apply dimension reduction before running this greedy algorithm. This avoids linear programming altogether in the first step in the above algorithm, and the second step can also be implemented quickly, because it involves projecting a point into a $k - 1$-dimensional simplex.

2.4 Topic Models

In this section, we will work with stochastic models to generate a collection of documents. These models are called *topic models*, and our goal is to learn their parameters. There is a wide range of types of topic models, but all of them fit into the following abstract framework:

Abstract Topic Model

Parameters: topic matrix $A \in \mathbb{R}^{m \times r}$, distribution μ on the simplex in $\mathbb{R}^r$

For $i = 1$ to n
    Sample W_i from μ
    Generate L words by sampling i.i.d. from the distribution AW_i
End

This procedure generates n documents of length L, and our goal is to infer A (and μ) from observing samples from this model. Let $\widetilde{M}$ be the observed term-by-document matrix. We will use this notation to distinguish it from its expectation

$$\mathbb{E}[\widetilde{M}|W] = M = AW.$$

In the case of nonnegative matrix factorization, we were given M and not $\widetilde{M}$. However, these matrices can be quite far apart! Hence, even though each document is described as a distribution on words, we only have partial knowledge of this distribution in the form of L samples from it. Our goal is to design algorithms that provably work even in these challenging models.

Now is a good time to point out that this model contains many well-studied topic models as a special case. All of them correspond to different choices of μ, the distribution that is used to generate the columns of W. Some of the most popular variants are:

(a) **Pure Topic Model:** Each document is about only one topic, hence μ is a distribution on the vertices of the simplex and each column in W has exactly one nonzero.

(b) **Latent Dirichlet Allocation [36]:** μ is a Dirichlet distribution. In particular, one can generate a sample from a Dirichlet distribution by taking independent samples from r (not necessarily identical) gamma distributions and then renormalizing so that their sum is one. This topic model allows documents to be about more than one topic, but its parameters are generally set so that it favors relatively sparse vectors W_i.

(c) **Correlated Topic Model [35]:** Certain pairs of topics are allowed to be positively or negatively correlated, and μ is constrained to be log-normal.

(d) **Pachinko Allocation Model [105]:** This is a multilevel generalization of LDA that allows for certain types of structured correlations.

In this section, we will use our algorithm for separable nonnegative matrix factorization to provably learn the parameters of a topic model for (essentially) any topic model where the topic matrix is separable. Thus this algorithm will work even in the presence of complex relationships between the topics.

The Gram Matrix

In this subsection, we will introduce two matrices, G and R, which we will call the Gram matrix and the topic co-occurrence matrix, respectively. The entries of these matrices will be defined in terms of the probability of various events. And throughout this section, we will always have the following experiment in mind: We generate a document from the abstract topic model, and let w_1 and w_2 denote the random variables for its first and second word, respectively. With this experiment in mind, we can define the Gram matrix:

Definition 2.4.1 *Let G denote the $m \times m$ matrix where*

$$G_{j,j'} = \mathbb{P}[w_1 = j, w_2 = j'].$$

Moreover, for each word, instead of sampling from AW_i, we can sample from W_i to choose which column of A to sample from. This procedure still generates a random sample from the same distribution AW_i, but each word $w_1 = j$ is annotated with the topic from which it came, $t_1 = i$ (i.e., the column of A we sampled it from). We can now define the topic co-occurrence matrix:

Definition 2.4.2 *Let R denote the $r \times r$ matrix where*

$$R_{i,i'} = \mathbb{P}[t_1 = i, t_2 = i'].$$

Note that we can estimate the entries of G directly from our samples, but we cannot directly estimate the entries of R. Nevertheless, these matrices are related according to the following identity:

Lemma 2.4.3 $G = ARA^T$

Proof: We have

$$G_{j,j'} = \mathbb{P}[w_1 = j, w_2 = j'] = \sum_{i,i'} \mathbb{P}[w_1 = j, w_2 = j' | t_1 = i, t_2 = i'] \mathbb{P}[t_1 = i, t_2 = i']$$

$$= \sum_{i,i'} \mathbb{P}[w_1 = j | t_1 = i] \mathbb{P}[w_2 = j' | t_2 = i'] \mathbb{P}[t_1 = i, t_2 = i']$$

$$= \sum_{i,i'} A_{j,i} A_{j',i'} R_{i,i'}$$

where the second-to-last line follows, because conditioned on their topics, w_1 and w_2 are sampled independently from the corresponding columns of A. This completes the proof. ∎

The crucial observation is that $G = A(RA^T)$ where A is separable and RA^T is nonnegative. Hence if we renormalize the rows of G to sum to one, the anchor words will be the extreme points of the convex hull of all of the rows and we can identify them through our algorithm for separable nonnegative matrix factorization. Can we infer the rest of A?

Recovery via Bayes's Rule

Consider the posterior distribution $\mathbb{P}[t_1 | w_1 = j]$. This is the posterior distribution on which topic generated $w_1 = j$ when you know nothing else about the document. The posterior distributions are just renormalizations of A so that the rows sum to one. Then suppose j is an anchor word for topic i. We will use the notation $j = \pi(i)$. It is easy to see

$$\mathbb{P}[t_1 = i' | w_1 = \pi(i)] = \begin{cases} 1, & \text{if } i' = i \\ 0 \text{ else.} \end{cases}$$

Now we can expand:

$$\mathbb{P}[w_1 = j | w_2 = j'] = \sum_{i'} \mathbb{P}[w_1 = j | w_2 = j', t_2 = i'] \mathbb{P}[t_2 = i' | w_2 = j']$$

$$= \sum_{i'} \mathbb{P}[w_1 = j | t_2 = i'] \mathbb{P}[t_2 = i' | w_2 = j']$$

In the last line we used the following identity:

Claim 2.4.4 $\mathbb{P}[w_1 = j | w_2 = j', t_2 = i'] = \mathbb{P}[w_1 = j | t_2 = i']$

We leave the proof of this claim as an exercise. We will also use the identity below:

Claim 2.4.5 $\mathbb{P}[w_1 = j | t_2 = i'] = \mathbb{P}[w_1 = j | w_2 = \pi(i')]$

Proof:

$$\mathbb{P}[w_1 = j | w_2 = \pi(i')] = \sum_{i''} \mathbb{P}[w_1 = j | w_2 = \pi(i'), t_2 = i''] \mathbb{P}[t_2 = i'' | w_2 = \pi(i')]$$

$$= \mathbb{P}[w_1 = j | w_2 = \pi(i'), t_2 = i']$$

where the last line follows, because the posterior distribution on the topic $t_2 = i''$, given that w_2 is an anchor word for topic i', is equal to one if and only if $i'' = i'$. Finally, the proof follows by invoking Claim 2.4.4. ∎

Now we can proceed:

$$\mathbb{P}[w_1 = j | w_2 = j'] = \sum_{i'} \mathbb{P}[w_1 = j | w_2 = \pi(i')] \underbrace{\mathbb{P}[t_2 = i' | w_2 = j']}_{\text{unknowns}}$$

Hence this is a linear system in variables $\mathbb{P}[w_1 = j | w_2 = \pi(i')]$ and it is not hard to show that if R has full rank, then it has a unique solution.

Finally, by Bayes's rule we can compute the entries of A:

$$\mathbb{P}[w = j | t = i] = \frac{\mathbb{P}[t = i | w = j] \mathbb{P}[w = j]}{\mathbb{P}[t = i]}$$

$$= \frac{\mathbb{P}[t = i | w = j] \mathbb{P}[w = j]}{\sum_{j'} \mathbb{P}[t = i | w = j'] \mathbb{P}[w = j']}$$

And putting it all together, we have the following algorithm:

Recover [14], [12]

Input: term-by-document matrix $M \in \mathbb{R}^{n \times m}$
Output: A, R

Compute the Gram matrix G
Compute the anchor words via **Separable NMF**
Solve for $\mathbb{P}[t = i | w = j]$
Compute $\mathbb{P}[w = j | t = i]$ from Bayes's rule

Theorem 2.4.6 *[14] There is a polynomial time algorithm to learn the topic matrix for any separable topic model, provided that R is full rank.*

Remark 2.4.7 *The running time and sample complexity of this algorithm depend polynomially on $m, n, r, \sigma_{min}(R), p, 1/\epsilon, \log 1/\delta$ where p is a lower bound on the probability of each anchor word, ϵ is the target accuracy, and δ is the failure probability.*

Note that this algorithm works for short documents, even for $L = 2$.

Experimental Results

Now we have provable algorithms for nonnegative matrix factorization and topic modeling under separability. But are *natural* topic models separable or close to being separable? Consider the following experiment:

(1) **UCI Dataset**: A collection of $300,000$ *New York Times* articles
(2) **MALLET**: A popular topic-modeling toolkit

We trained MALLET on the UCI dataset and found that with $r = 200$, about 0.9 fraction of the topics had a near anchor word – i.e., a word where $\mathbb{P}[t = i | w = j]$ had a value of at least 0.9 on some topic. Indeed, the algorithms we gave can be shown to work in the presence of some modest amount of error – deviation from the assumption of separability. But can they work with this much modeling error?

We then ran the following additional experiment:

(1) Run MALLET on the UCI dataset, learn a topic matrix ($r = 200$).
(2) Use A to generate a new set of documents synthetically from an LDA model.

(3) Run MALLET and our algorithm on a new set of documents, and compare their outputs to the ground truth. In particular, compute the minimum cost matching between the columns of the estimate and the columns of the ground truth.

It is important to remark that this is a biased experiment – biased *against* our algorithm! We are comparing how well we can find the hidden topics (in a setting where the topic matrix is only close to separable) to how well MALLET can find its own output again. And with enough documents, we can find it more accurately and hundreds of times faster! This new algorithm enables us to explore much larger collections of documents than ever before.

2.5 Exercises

Problem 2-1: Which of the following are equivalent definitions of nonnegative rank? For each, give a proof or a counterexample.

(a) The smallest r such that M can be written as the sum of r rank-one nonnegative matrices

(b) The smallest r such that there are r nonnegative vectors $v_1, v_2, \ldots, v_r$ such that the cone generated by them contains all the columns of M

(c) The largest r such that there are r columns of M, $M_1, M_2, \ldots, M_r$ such that no column in the set is contained in the cone generated by the remaining $r - 1$ columns

Problem 2-2: Let $M \in \mathbb{R}^{n \times n}$ where $M_{i,j} = (i - j)^2$. Prove that $\text{rank}(M) = 3$ and that $\text{rank}^+(M) \geq \log_2 n$. *Hint:* To prove a lower bound on $\text{rank}^+(M)$, it suffices to consider just where it is zero and where it is nonzero.

Problem 2-3: Papadimitriou et al. [118] considered the following document model: $M = AW$ and each column of W has only one nonzero and the support of each column of A is disjoint. Prove that the left singular vectors of M are the columns of A (after rescaling). You may assume that all the nonzero singular values of M are distinct. *Hint:* MM^T is a block diagonal after applying a permutation π to its rows and columns.

Problem 2-4: Consider the following algorithm:

Greedy Anchor Words [13]

Input: matrix $M \in \mathbb{R}^{n \times m}$ satisfying the conditions in Theorem 2.3.12
Output: A, W

Set $S = \emptyset$
For $i = 2$ to r
      Project the rows of M orthogonal to the span of vectors in S
      Add the row with the largest ℓ_2 norm to S
End

Let $M = AW$ where A is separable and the *rows* of M, A, and W are normalized to sum to one. Also assume W has full row rank. Prove that Greedy Anchor Words finds all the anchor words and nothing else. *Hint:* the ℓ_2 norm is strictly convex — i.e., for any $x \neq y$ and $t \in (0, 1)$, $\|tx + (1 - t)y\|_2 < t\|x\|_2 + (1 - t)\|y\|_2$.

3
Tensor Decompositions
Algorithms

In this chapter, we will study tensors and various structural and computational problems we can ask about them. Generally, many problems that are easy over matrices become ill-posed or *NP*-hard when working over tensors instead. Contrary to popular belief, this isn't a reason to pack up your bags and go home. Actually, there are things we can get out of tensors that we can't get out of matrices. We just have to be careful about what types of problems we try to solve. More precisely, in this chapter we will give an algorithm with provable guarantees for low-rank tensor decomposition – that works in natural but restricted settings – as well as some preliminary applications of it to factor analysis.

3.1 The Rotation Problem

Before we study the algorithmic problems surrounding tensors, let's first understand why they're useful. To do this, we'll need to introduce the concept of *factor analysis*, where working with tensors instead of matrices will help us circumvent one of the major stumbling blocks. So, what is factor analysis? It's a basic tool in statistics where the goal is to take many variables and explain them away using a much smaller number of hidden variables, called factors. But it's best to understand it through an example. And why not start with a historical example? It was first used in the pioneering work of Charles Spearman, who had a theory about the nature of intelligence – he believed that there are fundamentally two types of intelligence: *mathematical* and *verbal*. I don't agree, but let's continue anyway.

He devised the following experiment to test out his theory: He measured the performance of one thousand students, each on ten different tests, and arranged his data into a 1000×10 matrix M. He believed that how a student performed on a given test was determined by some hidden variables that had to do with the student and the test. Imagine that each student is described by a two-dimensional vector where the two coordinates give numerical scores quantifying his or her mathematical and verbal intelligence, respectively. Similarly, imagine that each test is also described by a two-dimensional vector, but the coordinates represent the extent to which it tests mathematical and verbal reasoning. Spearman set out to find this set of two-dimensional vectors, one for each student and one for each test, so that how a student performs on a test is given by the inner product between their two respective vectors.

Let's translate the problem into a more convenient language. What we are looking for is a particular factorization

$$M = AB^T$$

where A is size 1000×2 and B is size 10×2 that validates Spearman's theory. The trouble is, even if there is a factorization $M = AB^T$ where the columns of A and the rows of B can be given some *meaningful* interpretation (that would corroborate Spearman's theory) how can we find it? There can be many other factorizations of M that have the same inner dimension but are not the factors we are looking for. To make this concrete, suppose that O is a 2×2 orthogonal matrix. Then we can write

$$M = AB^T = (AO)(O^T B^T)$$

and we can just as easily find the factorization $M = \hat{A}\hat{B}^T$ where $\hat{A} = AO$ and $\hat{B} = BO$ instead. So even if there is a meaningful factorization that would explain our data, there is no guarantee that we find it, and in general what we find might be an arbitrary inner rotation of it that itself is difficult to interpret. This is called the *rotation problem*. This is the stumbling block that we alluded to earlier, which we encounter if we use matrix techniques to perform factor analysis.

What went wrong here is that low-rank matrix decompositions are not unique. Let's elaborate on what exactly we mean by unique in this context. Suppose we are given a matrix M and are promised that it has some meaningful low-rank decomposition

$$M = \sum_{i=1}^{r} a^{(i)} (b^{(i)})^T.$$

Our goal is to recover the factors $a^{(i)}$ and $b^{(i)}$. The trouble is that we could compute the singular value decomposition $M = U\Sigma V^T$ and find another low-rank decomposition

$$M = \sum_{i=1}^{r} \sigma_i u^{(i)} (v^{(i)})^T.$$

These are potentially two very different sets of factors that just happen to recreate the same matrix. In fact, the vectors $u^{(i)}$ are necessarily orthonormal, because they came from the singular value decomposition, even though there is a priori no reason to think that the true factors $a^{(i)}$ that we are looking for are orthonormal too. So now we can qualitatively answer the question we posed at the outset. Why are we interested in tensors? It's because they solve the rotation problem and their decomposition is unique under much weaker conditions than their matrix decomposition counterparts.

3.2 A Primer on Tensors

A tensor might sound mysterious, but it's just a collection of numbers. Let's start with the case we'll spend most of our time on. A third-order tensor T has three dimensions, sometimes called *rows*, *columns*, and *tubes*. If the size of T is $n_1 \times n_2 \times n_3$, then the standard notation is that $T_{i,j,k}$ refers to the number in row i, column j, and tube k in T. Now, a matrix is just a second-order tensor, because it's a collection of numbers indexed by two indices. And of course you can consider tensors of any order you'd like.

We can think about tensors many different ways, and all of these viewpoints will be useful at different points in this chapter. Perhaps the simplest way to think of an order-three tensor T is as nothing more than a collection of n_3 matrices, each of size $n_1 \times n_2$, that are stacked on top of each other. Before we go any further, we should define the notion of the rank of a tensor. This will allow us to explore when a tensor is not just a collection of matrices, as well as when and how these matrices are interrelated.

Definition 3.2.1 *A rank-one, third-order tensor T is the tensor product of three vectors u, v, and w, and its entries are*

$$T_{i,j,k} = u_i v_j w_k.$$

Thus if the dimensions of u, v, and w are n_1, n_2, and n_3, respectively, T is of size $n_1 \times n_2 \times n_3$. Moreover, we will often use the following shorthand:

$$T = u \otimes v \otimes w$$

We can now define the rank of a tensor:

Definition 3.2.2 *The rank of a third-order tensor T is the smallest integer r so that we can write*

$$T = \sum_{i=1}^{r} u^{(i)} \otimes v^{(i)} \otimes w^{(i)}.$$

Recall, the rank of a matrix M is the smallest integer r so that M can be written as the sum of r rank-one matrices. The beauty of the rank of a matrix is how many equivalent definitions it admits. What we have above is the natural generalization of one of the many definitions of the rank of a matrix to tensors. The decomposition above is often called a CANDECOMP/PARAFAC decomposition.

Now that we have the definition of rank in hand, let's understand how a low-rank tensor is not *just* an arbitrary collection of low-rank matrices. Let $T_{.,.,k}$ denote the $n_1 \times n_2$ matrix corresponding to the kth slice through the tensor.

Claim 3.2.3 *Consider a rank-r tensor*

$$T = \sum_{i=1}^{r} u^{(i)} \otimes v^{(i)} \otimes w^{(i)}.$$

Then for all $1 \leq k \leq n_3$,

$$colspan(T_{.,.,k}) \subseteq span(\{u^{(i)}\}_i)$$

and moreover,

$$rowspan(T_{.,.,k}) \subseteq span(\{v^{(i)}\}_i).$$

We leave the proof as an exercise for the reader. Actually, this claim tells us why not every stacking of low-rank matrices yields a low-rank tensor. True, if we take a low-rank tensor and look at its n_3 different slices, we get matrices of dimension $n_1 \times n_2$ with rank at most r. But we know more than that. Each of their column spaces is contained in the span of the vectors $u^{(i)}$. Similarly, their row spaces are contained in the span of the vectors $v^{(i)}$.

Intuitively, the rotation problem comes from the fact that a matrix is just one *view* of the vectors $\{u^{(i)}\}_i$ and $\{v^{(i)}\}_i$. But a tensor gives us multiple views through each of its slices, which helps us resolve the indeterminacy. If this doesn't quite make sense yet, that's all right. Come back to it once you understand Jennrich's algorithm and think about it again.

The Trouble with Tensors

Before we proceed, it will be important to dispel any myths you might have that working with tensors will be a straightforward generalization of working with matrices. So, what is so subtle about working with tensors? For starters, what makes linear algebra so elegant and appealing is how something like the rank of a matrix M admits a number of equivalent definitions. When we defined the rank of a tensor, we were careful to say that what we were doing was taking *one* of the definitions of the rank of a matrix and writing down the natural generalization to tensors. But what if we took a different definition for the rank of a matrix and generalized it in the natural way? Would we get the same notion of rank for a tensor? Usually not!

Let's try it out. Instead of defining the rank of a matrix M as the smallest number of rank-one matrices we need to add up to get M, we could define the rank through the dimension of its column/row space. This next claim just says that we'd get the same notion of rank.

Claim 3.2.4 *The rank of a matrix M is equal to the dimension of its column/row space. More precisely,*

$$rank(M) = dim(colspan(M)) = dim(rowspan(M)).$$

Does this relation hold for tensors? Not even close! As a simple example, let's set $n_1 = k^2$, $n_2 = k$, and $n_3 = k$. Then, if we take the n_1 columns of T to be the columns of a $k^2 \times k^2$ identity matrix, we know that the $n_2 n_3$ columns of T are all linearly independent and have dimension k^2. But the $n_1 n_3$ rows of T have dimension at most k because they live in a k-dimensional space. So for tensors, the dimension of the span of the rows is not necessarily equal to the dimension of the span of the columns/tubes.

Things are only going to get worse from here. There are some nasty subtleties about the rank of a tensor. First, the field is important. Let's suppose T is real-valued. We defined the rank as the smallest value of r so that we can write T as the sum of r rank-one tensors. But should we allow these tensors to have complex values, or only real values? Actually this *can* change the rank, as the following example illustrates.

Consider the following $2 \times 2 \times 2$ tensor:

$$T = \begin{bmatrix} 1 & 0 \\ 0 & 1 \end{bmatrix}; \begin{bmatrix} 0 & -1 \\ 1 & 0 \end{bmatrix}$$

where the first 2×2 matrix is the first slice through the tensor and the second 2×2 matrix is the second slice. It is not hard to show that $rank_{\mathbb{R}}(T) \geq 3$. But it is easy to check that

$$T = \frac{1}{2} \left(\begin{bmatrix} 1 \\ -i \end{bmatrix} \otimes \begin{bmatrix} 1 \\ i \end{bmatrix} \otimes \begin{bmatrix} 1 \\ -i \end{bmatrix} + \begin{bmatrix} 1 \\ i \end{bmatrix} \otimes \begin{bmatrix} 1 \\ -i \end{bmatrix} \otimes \begin{bmatrix} 1 \\ i \end{bmatrix} \right).$$

So even though T is real-valued, it can be written as the sum of *fewer* rank-one tensors if we are allowed to use complex numbers. This issue never arises for matrices. If M is real-valued and there is a way to write it as the sum of r rank-one matrices with (possibly) complex-valued entries, there is always a way to write it as the sum of at most r rank-one matrices, all of whose entries are real. This seems like a happy accident, now that we are faced with objects whose rank is field-dependent.

Another worrisome issue is that there are tensors of rank three that can be arbitrarily well-approximated by tensors of rank two. This leads us to the definition of border rank:

Definition 3.2.5 *The* border rank *of a tensor T is the minimum r such that for any $\epsilon > 0$ there is a rank-r tensor that is entrywise ϵ-close to T.*

For matrices, the rank and border rank are the same! If we fix a matrix M with rank r, then there is a finite limit (depending on M) to how well we can approximate it by a rank $r' < r$ matrix. One can deduce this from the optimality of the truncated singular value decomposition for low-rank approximation. But for tensors, the rank and border rank can indeed be different, as our final example illustrates.

Consider the following $2 \times 2 \times 2$ tensor:

$$T = \begin{bmatrix} 0 & 1 \\ 1 & 0 \end{bmatrix}; \begin{bmatrix} 1 & 0 \\ 0 & 0 \end{bmatrix}$$

It is not hard to show that $\mathrm{rank}_{\mathbb{R}}(T) \geq 3$. Yet it admits an arbitrarily good rank-two approximation using the following scheme. Let

$$S_n = \begin{bmatrix} n & 1 \\ 1 & \frac{1}{n} \end{bmatrix}; \begin{bmatrix} 1 & \frac{1}{n} \\ \frac{1}{n} & \frac{1}{n^2} \end{bmatrix} \text{ and } R_n = \begin{bmatrix} n & 0 \\ 0 & 0 \end{bmatrix}; \begin{bmatrix} 0 & 0 \\ 0 & 0 \end{bmatrix}.$$

Both S_n and R_n are rank one, and so $S_n - R_n$ has rank at most two. But notice that $S_n - R_n$ is entrywise $1/n$-close to T, and as we increase n we get an arbitrarily good approximation to T. So even though T has rank three, its border rank is at most two. You can see this example takes advantage of larger and larger cancellations. It also shows that the magnitude of the entries of the best low-rank approximation cannot be bounded as a function of the magnitude of the entries in T.

A useful property of matrices is that the best rank k approximation to M can be obtained directly from its best rank $k + 1$ approximation. More precisely, suppose that $B^{(k)}$ and $B^{(k+1)}$ are, respectively, the best rank k and rank $k + 1$ approximations to M in terms of, say, Frobenius norm. Then we can obtain $B^{(k)}$ as the best rank k approximation to $B^{(k+1)}$. However, for tensors, the best rank

k and rank $k + 1$ approximations to T need not share *any* common rank-one terms at all. The best rank k approximation to a tensor is unwieldy. You have to worry about its field. You cannot bound the magnitude of its entries in terms of the input. And it changes in complex ways as you vary k.

To me, the most serious issue at the root of all of this is computational complexity. Of course the rank of a tensor is not equal to the dimension of its column space. The former is *NP*-hard (by a result of Hastad [85]) and the latter is easy to compute. You have to be careful with tensors. In fact, computational complexity is such a pervasive issue, with so many problems that are easy to compute on matrices turning out to be *NP*-hard on tensors, that the title of a well-known paper of Hillar and Lim [86] sums it up: "Most Tensor Problems Are Hard."

To back this up, Hillar and Lim [86] proved that a laundry list of other problems, such as finding the best low-rank approximation, computing the spectral norm, and deciding whether a tensor is nonnegative definite, are *NP*-hard too. If this section is a bit pessimistic for you, keep in mind that all I'm trying to do is set the stage so you'll be as excited as you should be — that there actually is something we can do with tensors!

3.3 Jennrich's Algorithm

In this section, we will introduce an algorithm for computing a minimum rank decomposition that works in a natural but restricted setting. This algorithm is called Jennrich's algorithm. Interestingly, it has been rediscovered numerous times (for reasons that we will speculate on later), and to the best of our knowledge the first place that it appeared was in a working paper of Harshman [84], where the author credits it to Dr. Robert Jennrich.

In what follows, we will assume we are given a tensor T, which we will assume has the following form:

$$T = \sum_{i=1}^{r} u^{(i)} \otimes v^{(i)} \otimes w^{(i)}$$

We will refer to the factors $u^{(i)}$, $v^{(i)}$, and $w^{(i)}$ as the *hidden* factors to emphasize that we do not know them but want to find them. We should be careful here. What do we mean by find them? There are some ambiguities that we can never hope to resolve. We can only hope to recover the factors up to an arbitrary reordering (of the sum) and up to certain rescalings that leave the rank-one tensors themselves unchanged. This motivates the following definition, which takes into account these issues:

Definition 3.3.1 *We say that two sets of factors*

$$\left\{(u^{(i)}, v^{(i)}, w^{(i)})\right\}_{i=1}^{r} \text{ and } \left\{(\hat{u}^{(i)}, \hat{v}^{(i)}, \hat{w}^{(i)})\right\}_{i=1}^{r}$$

are equivalent if there is a permutation $\pi : [r] \to [r]$ *such that for all* i

$$u^{(i)} \otimes v^{(i)} \otimes w^{(i)} = \hat{u}^{(\pi(i))} \otimes \hat{v}^{(\pi(i))} \otimes \hat{w}^{(\pi(i))}.$$

The important point is that two sets of factors that are equivalent produce two decompositions

$$T = \sum_{i=1}^{r} u^{(i)} \otimes v^{(i)} \otimes w^{(i)} = \sum_{i=1}^{r} \hat{u}^{(i)} \otimes \hat{v}^{(i)} \otimes \hat{w}^{(i)}$$

that have the same set of rank-one tensors in their sums.

The main question in this section is: Given T, can we efficiently find a set of factors that are equivalent to the hidden factors? We will state and prove a version of Jennrich's algorithm that is more general, following the approach of Leurgans, Ross, and Abel [103].

Theorem 3.3.2 *[84], [103] Suppose we are given a tensor of the form*

$$T = \sum_{i=1}^{r} u^{(i)} \otimes v^{(i)} \otimes w^{(i)}$$

where the following conditions are met:

(1) the vectors $\{u^{(i)}\}_i$ *are linearly independent,*
(2) the vectors $\{v^{(i)}\}_i$ *are linearly independent, and*
(3) every pair of vectors in $\{w^{(i)}\}_i$ *is linearly independent.*

Then there is an efficient algorithm to find a decomposition

$$T = \sum_{i=1}^{r} \hat{u}^{(i)} \otimes \hat{v}^{(i)} \otimes \hat{w}^{(i)}$$

and moreover, the factors $(u^{(i)}, v^{(i)}, w^{(i)})$ *and* $(\hat{u}^{(i)}, \hat{v}^{(i)}, \hat{w}^{(i)})$ *are equivalent.*

The original result of Jennrich [84] was stated as a *uniqueness* theorem, that under the conditions on the factors $u^{(i)}$, $v^{(i)}$, and $w^{(i)}$ above, *any* decomposition of T into at most r rank-one tensors must use an equivalent set of factors. It just so happened that the way that Jennrich proved this uniqueness theorem was by giving an algorithm that finds the decomposition, although in the paper it was never stated that way. Intriguingly, this seems to be a major contributor to why the result was forgotten. Much of the subsequent literature cited a stronger uniqueness theorem of Kruskal, whose proof is nonconstructive, and seemed to forget that the weaker uniqueness theorem of Jennrich comes along with an algorithm. Let this be a word of warning: If you not only prove some mathematical fact but your argument readily yields an algorithm, then say so!

Jennrich's Algorithm [84]

Input: tensor $T \in \mathbb{R}^{m \times n \times p}$ satisfying the conditions in Theorem 3.3.2
Output: factors $\{u_i\}_i$, $\{v_i\}_i$, and $\{w_i\}_i$

Choose $a, b \in \mathbb{S}^{p-1}$ uniformly at random; set

$$T^{(a)} = \sum_{i=1}^{p} a_i T_{\cdot,\cdot,i} \text{ and } T^{(b)} = \sum_{i=1}^{p} b_i T_{\cdot,\cdot,i}$$

Compute the eigendecomposition of $T^{(a)}(T^{(b)})^{+}$ and $((T^{(a)})^{+}T^{(b)})^{T}$

  Let U and V be the eigenvectors corresponding to nonzero eigenvalues

  Pair up $u^{(i)}$ and $v^{(i)}$ iff their eigenvalues are reciprocals

Solve for $w^{(i)}$ in $T = \sum_{i=1}^{r} u^{(i)} \otimes v^{(i)} \otimes w^{(i)}$

End

Recall that $T_{\cdot,\cdot,i}$ denotes the ith matrix slice through T. Thus $T^{(a)}$ is just the weighted sum of matrix slices through T, each weighted by a_i.

The first step in the analysis is to express $T^{(a)}$ and $T^{(b)}$ in terms of the hidden factors. Let U and V be size $m \times r$ and $n \times r$ matrices, respectively, whose columns are $u^{(i)}$ and $v^{(i)}$. Let $D^{(a)}$ and $D^{(b)}$ be $r \times r$ diagonal matrices whose entries are $\langle w^{(i)}, a \rangle$ and $\langle w^{(i)}, b \rangle$, respectively. Then

Lemma 3.3.3 $T^{(a)} = UD^{(a)}V^{T}$ and $T^{(b)} = UD^{(b)}V^{T}$

Proof: Since the operation of computing $T^{(a)}$ from T is linear, we can apply it to each of the rank-one tensors in the low-rank decomposition of T. It is easy to see that if we are given the rank-one tensor $u \otimes v \otimes w$, then the effect of taking the weighted sum of matrix slices, where the ith slice is weighted by a_i, is that we obtain the matrix $\langle w, a \rangle u \otimes v$.

Thus by linearity we have

$$T^{(a)} = \sum_{i=1}^{r} \langle w^{(i)}, a \rangle u^{(i)} \otimes v^{(i)}$$

which yields the first part of the lemma. The second part follows analogously with a replaced by b. ∎

It turns out that we can now recover the columns of U and the columns of V through a generalized eigendecomposition. Let's do a thought experiment. If we are given a matrix M of the form $M = UDU^{-1}$ where the entries along the diagonal matrix D are distinct and nonzero, the columns of U will be eigenvectors, except that they are not necessarily unit vectors. Since the entries of D are distinct, the eigendecomposition of M is unique, and this means we can recover the columns of U (up to rescaling) as the eigenvectors of M.

Now, if we are instead given two matrices of the form $A = UD^{(a)}V^T$ and $B = UD^{(b)}V^T$, then if the entries of $D^{(a)}(D^{(b)})^{-1}$ are distinct and nonzero, we can recover the columns of U and V (again up to rescaling) through an eigendecomposition of

$$AB^{-1} = UD^{(a)}(D^{(b)})^{-1}U^{-1} \text{ and } (A^{-1}B)^T = VD^{(b)}(D^{(a)})^{-1}V^{-1}$$

respectively. It turns out that instead of actually forming the matrices above, we could instead look for all the vectors v that satisfy $Av = \lambda_v Bv$, which is called a generalized eigendecomposition. In any case, this is the main idea behind the following lemma, although we need to take some care, since in our setting the matrices U an V are not necessarily square, let alone invertible matrices.

Lemma 3.3.4 *Almost surely, the columns of U and V are the unique eigenvectors corresponding to nonzero eigenvalues of $T^{(a)}(T^{(b)})^+$ and $((T^{(a)})^+T^{(b)})^T$, respectively. Moreover, the eigenvalue corresponding to $u^{(i)}$ is the reciprocal of the eigenvalue corresponding to $v^{(i)}$.*

Proof: We can use the formula for $T^{(a)}$ and $T^{(b)}$ in Lemma 3.3.3 to compute

$$T^{(a)}(T^{(b)})^+ = UD^{(a)}(D^{(b)})^+U^+$$

The entries of $D^{(a)}(D^{(b)})^+$ are $\langle w^{(i)}, a \rangle / \langle w^{(i)}, b \rangle$. Then, because every pair of vectors in $\{w^{(i)}\}_i$ is linearly independent, we have that almost surely over the choice of a and b, the entries along the diagonal of $D^{(a)}(D^{(b)})^+$ will all be nonzero and distinct.

Now, returning to the formula above for $T^{(a)}(T^{(b)})^+$, we see that it is an eigendecomposition and, moreover, that the nonzero eigenvalues are distinct. Thus the columns of U are the unique eigenvectors of $T^{(a)}(T^{(b)})^+$ with nonzero eigenvalue, and the eigenvalue corresponding to $u^{(i)}$ is $\langle w^{(i)}, a \rangle / \langle w^{(i)}, b \rangle$. An identical argument shows that the columns of V are the unique eigenvectors of

$$((T^{(a)})^+T^{(b)})^T = VD^{(b)}(D^{(a)})^+V^+$$

with nonzero eigenvalue. And by inspection, we have that the eigenvalue corresponding to $v^{(i)}$ is $\langle w^{(i)}, b \rangle / \langle w^{(i)}, a \rangle$, which completes the proof of the lemma. ■

Now, to complete the proof of the theorem, notice that we have only recovered the columns of U and the columns of V up to rescaling – i.e., for each column, we recovered the corresponding unit vector. We will push this rescaling factor in with the missing factors $w^{(i)}$. Thus the linear system in the last step of the algorithm clearly has a solution, and what remains is to prove that this is its only solution.

Lemma 3.3.5 *The matrices* $\left\{ u^{(i)} (v^{(i)})^T \right\}_{i=1}^{r}$ *are linearly independent.*

Proof: Suppose (for the sake of contradiction) that there is a collection of coefficients that are not all zero where

$$\sum_{i=1}^{r} \alpha_i u^{(i)} (v^{(i)})^T = 0.$$

Suppose (without loss of generality) that $\alpha_1 \neq 0$. Because by assumption the vectors $\{v^{(i)}\}_i$ are linearly independent, we have that there is a vector a that satisfies that $\langle v^{(1)}, a \rangle \neq 0$ but is orthogonal to all other $v^{(i)}$s. Now, if we right multiply the above identity by a, we get

$$\alpha_1 \langle v^{(1)}, a \rangle u^{(1)} = 0$$

which is a contradiction, because the left-hand side is nonzero. ■

This immediately implies that the linear system over the $w^{(i)}$'s has a unique solution. We can write the linear system as an $mn \times r$ matrix, each of whose columns represents a matrix $u^{(i)} (v^{(i)})^T$ but in vector form, times an unknown $r \times p$ matrix whose columns represent the vectors $w^{(i)}$. The product of these two matrices is constrained to be equal to an $mn \times p$ matrix whose columns represent each of the p matrix slices through the tensor T, but again in vector form. This completes the proof of Theorem 3.3.2.

If you want a nice open question, note that the conditions in Jennrich's algorithm can only ever hold if $r \leq \min(n_1, n_2)$, because we need that the vectors $\{u^{(i)}\}_i$ and $\{v^{(i)}\}_i$ are linearly independent. This is called the undercomplete case, because the rank is bounded by the largest dimension of the tensor. When r is larger than either n_1, n_2, or n_3, we know that the decomposition of T is generically unique. But are there algorithms for decomposing generic overcomplete third-order tensors? This question is open even when $r = 1.1 \max(n_1, n_2, n_3)$.

3.4 Perturbation Bounds

This section is good medicine. What we have so far is an algorithm (Jennrich's algorithm) that decomposes a third-order tensor T under some natural conditions on the factors, but under the assumption that we know T *exactly*. In our applications, this just won't be enough. We'll need to handle noise. The aim of this section is to answer the question: If we are given $\widetilde{T} = T + E$ instead (you can think of E as representing sampling noise), how well can we approximate the hidden factors?

Our algorithm won't change. We will still use Jennrich's algorithm. Rather, what we want to do in this section is track how the errors propagate. We want to give quantitative bounds on how well we approximate the hidden factors, and the bounds we give will depend on E and properties of T. The main step in Jennrich's algorithm is to compute an eigendecomposition. Naturally, this is where we will spend most of our time – in understanding when eigendecompositions are stable. From this, we will easily be able to see when and why Jennrich's algorithm works in the presence of noise.

Prerequisites for Perturbation Bounds

Now let's be more precise. The main question we're interested in is the following:

Question 5 *If $M = UDU^{-1}$ is diagonalizable and we are given $\widetilde{M} = M + E$, how well can we estimate U?*

The natural thing to do is to compute a matrix that diagonalizes $\widetilde{M}$ – i.e., $\widetilde{U}$, where $\widetilde{M} = \widetilde{U}\widetilde{D}\widetilde{U}^{-1}$ – and quantify how good $\widetilde{U}$ is as an estimate for U. But before we dive right in, it's good to do a thought experiment.

There are some cases where it just is not possible to say that U and $\widetilde{U}$ are close. For example, if there are two eigenvalues of M that are very close to each other, then the perturbation E could in principle collapse two eigenvectors into a single two-dimensional eigenspace, and we would never be able to estimate the columns of U. What this means is that our perturbation bounds will have to depend on the minimum separation between any pair of eigenvalues of M.

Just like this, there is one more thought experiment we can do, which tells us another property of M that must make its way into our perturbation bounds. But before we get there, let's understand the issue in a simpler setup. This takes us to an important notion from numerical linear algebra.

Definition 3.4.1 *The* condition number *of a matrix U is defined as*

$$\kappa(U) = \frac{\sigma_{\max}(U)}{\sigma_{\min}(U)}$$

where $\sigma_{\max}(U)$ and $\sigma_{\min}(U)$ are the maximum and minimum singular values of U, respectively.

The condition number captures how errors amplify when solving systems of linear equations. Let's be more precise: Consider the problem of solving for x in $Mx = b$. Suppose we are given M exactly, but we only know an estimate $\tilde{b} = b + e$ of b. How well can we approximate x?

Question 6 *If we obtain a solution $\tilde{x}$ that satisfies $M\tilde{x} = \tilde{b}$, how close is $\tilde{x}$ to x?*

We have $\tilde{x} = M^{-1}\tilde{b} = x + M^{-1}e = x + M^{-1}(\tilde{b} - b)$. So

$$\|x - \tilde{x}\| \leq \frac{1}{\sigma_{\min}(M)}\|b - \tilde{b}\|.$$

Since $Mx = b$, we also have $\|b\| \leq \sigma_{\max}(M)\|x\|$. It follows that

$$\frac{\|x - \tilde{x}\|}{\|x\|} \leq \frac{\sigma_{\max}(M)}{\sigma_{\min}(M)}\frac{\|b - \tilde{b}\|}{\|b\|} = \kappa(M)\frac{\|b - \tilde{b}\|}{\|b\|}.$$

The term $\|b - \tilde{b}\|/\|b\|$ is often called the *relative error* and is a popular distance to measure closeness in numerical linear algebra. What the discussion above tells us is that the condition number controls the relative error when solving a linear system.

Now let's tie this back in to our earlier discussion. It turns out that our perturbation bounds for eigendecompositions will also have to depend on the condition number of U. Intuitively, this is because, given U and U^{-1}, finding the eigenvalues of M is like solving a linear system that depends on U and U^{-1}. This can be made more precise, but we won't do so here.

Gershgorin's Disk Theorem and Distinct Eigenvalues

Now that we understand what sorts of properties of M should make their way into our perturbation bounds, we can move on to actually proving them. The first question we need to answer is: Is $\tilde{M}$ diagonalizable? Our approach will be to show that if M has distinct eigenvalues and E is small enough, then $\tilde{M}$ also has distinct eigenvalues. The main tool in our proof will be a useful fact from numerical linear algebra called Gershgorin's disk theorem:

Theorem 3.4.2 *The eigenvalues of an $n \times n$ matrix M are all contained in the following union of disks in the complex plane:*

$$\bigcup_{i=1}^{n} D(M_{ii}, R_i)$$

where $D(a, b) := \{x \mid \|x - a\| \leq b\} \subseteq \mathbb{C}$ and $R_i = \sum_{j \neq i} |M_{ij}|$.

It is useful to think about this theorem in a special case. If $M = I + E$ where I is the identity matrix and E is a perturbation that has only small entries, Gershgorin's disk theorem is what tells us the intuitively obvious fact that the eigenvalues of M are all close to one. The radii in the theorem give quantitative bounds on how close to one they are. Now for the proof:

Proof: Let (x, λ) be an eigenvector-eigenvalue pair (note that this is valid even when M is not diagonalizable). Let i denote the coordinate of x with the maximum absolute value. Then $Mx = \lambda x$ gives $\sum_j M_{ij} x_j = \lambda x_i$. So $\sum_{j \neq i} M_{ij} x_j = \lambda x_i - M_{ii} x_i$. We conclude:

$$|\lambda - M_{ii}| = \left| \sum_{j \neq i} M_{ij} \frac{x_j}{x_i} \right| \leq \sum_{j \neq i} |M_{ij}| = R_i.$$

Thus $\lambda \in D(M_{ii}, R_i)$. ∎

Now we can return to the task of showing that $\widetilde{M}$ is diagonalizable. The idea is straightforward and comes from digesting a single expression. Consider

$$U^{-1} \widetilde{M} U = U^{-1} (M + E) U = D + U^{-1} E U.$$

What does this expression tell us? The right-hand side is a perturbation of a diagonal matrix, so we can use Gershgorin's disk theorem to say that its eigenvalues are close to those of D. Now, because left multiplying by U^{-1} and right multiplying by U is a similarity transformation, this in turn tells us about $\widetilde{M}$'s eigenvalues.

Let's put this plan into action and apply Gershgorin's disk theorem to understand the eigenvalues of $\widetilde{D} = D + U^{-1} E U$. First, we can bound the magnitude of the entries of $\widetilde{E} = U^{-1} E U$ as follows. Let $\|A\|_\infty$ denote the matrix max norm, which is the largest absolute value of any entry in A.

Lemma 3.4.3 $\|\widetilde{E}\|_\infty \leq \kappa(U) \|E\|$

Proof: For any i and j, we can regard $\widetilde{E}_{i,j}$ as the quadratic form of the ith row of U^{-1} and the jth column of U on E. Now, the jth column of U has Euclidean norm at most $\sigma_{max}(U)$, and similarly the ith row of U^{-1} has Euclidean norm at most $\sigma_{max}(U^{-1}) = 1/\sigma_{min}(U)$. Together, this yields the desired bound. ∎

Now let's prove that, under the appropriate conditions, the eigenvalues of $\widetilde{M}$ are distinct. Let $R = \max_i \sum_j |\widetilde{E}_{i,j}|$ and let $\delta = \min_{i \neq j} |D_{i,i} - D_{j,j}|$ be the minimum separation of the eigenvalues of D.

Lemma 3.4.4 *If $R < \delta/2$, then the eigenvalues of $\widetilde{M}$ are distinct.*

Proof: First we use Gershgorin's disk theorem to conclude that the eigenvalues of $\widetilde{D}$ are contained in disjoint disks, one for each row. There's a minor technicality, that Gershgorin's disk theorem works with a radius that is the sum of the absolute values of the entries in a row, except for the diagonal entry. But we leave it as an exercise to check that the calculation still goes through.

Actually, we are not done yet.[1] Even if Gershgorin's disk theorem implies that there are disjoint disks (one for each row) that contain the eigenvalues of $\widetilde{D}$, how do we know that no disk contains more than one eigenvalue and that no disk contains no eigenvalues? It turns out that the eigenvalues of a matrix are a continuous function of the entries, so as we trace out a path

$$\gamma(t) = (1 - t)D + t(\widetilde{D})$$

from D to $\widetilde{D}$ as t goes from zero to one, the disks in Gershgorin's disk theorem are always disjoint and no eigenvalue can jump from one disk to another. Thus, at $\widetilde{D}$ we know that there really is exactly one eigenvalue in each disk, and since the disks are disjoint, we have that the eigenvalues of $\widetilde{D}$ are distinct as desired. Of course the eigenvalues of $\widetilde{D}$ and $\widetilde{M}$ are the same, because they are related by a similarity transformation. ∎

Comparing the Eigendecompositions

We now know that $\widetilde{M}$ has distinct eigenvalues, so we are finally allowed to write $\widetilde{M} = \widetilde{U}\widetilde{D}\widetilde{U}^{-1}$, because $\widetilde{M}$ is diagonalizable. Let's turn to our final step. There is a natural correspondence between eigenvalues of M and eigenvalues of $\widetilde{M}$, because what the proof in the previous subsection told us was that there is a collection of disjoint disks that contains exactly one eigenvalue of M and exactly one eigenvalue of $\widetilde{M}$. So let's permute the eigenvectors of $\widetilde{M}$ to make our life notationally easier. In fact, why not make it easier still. Let's assume (without loss of generality) that all the eigenvectors are unit vectors.

---

[1] Thanks to Santosh Vempala for pointing out this gap in an earlier version of this book. See also [79].

Now suppose we are given $(\widetilde{u}_i, \widetilde{\lambda}_i)$ and (u_i, λ_i), which are corresponding eigenvector-eigenvalue pairs for $\widetilde{M}$ and M, respectively. Let $\sum_j c_j u_j = \widetilde{u}_i$. We know that there is a choice of c_j's that makes this expression hold, because the u_j's are a basis. What we want to show is that in this expression, c_j for all $j \neq i$ is small. This would imply that u_i and $\widetilde{u}_i$ are close.

Lemma 3.4.5 *For any $j \neq i$, we have*

$$|c_j| \leq \frac{\|E\|}{\sigma_{min}(U)(\delta - R)}.$$

Proof: We'll get this by manipulating the expression $\sum_j c_j u_j = \widetilde{u}_i$. First, multiplying both sides of the equation by $\widetilde{M}$ and using the fact that $\{u_i\}_i$ are eigenvectors of M and $\{\widetilde{u}_i\}_i$ are eigenvectors of $\widetilde{M}$, we get

$$\sum_j c_j \lambda_j u_j + E \widetilde{u}_i = \widetilde{\lambda}_i \widetilde{u}_i$$

which, rearranging terms, yields the expression $\sum_j c_j (\lambda_j - \widetilde{\lambda}_i) u_j = -E \widetilde{u}_i$.

Now what we want to do is pick out just one of the coefficients on the left-hand side and use the right-hand side to bound it. To do this, let w_j^T be the jth row of U^{-1}, and left multiplying both sides of the expression above by this vector, we obtain

$$c_j(\lambda_j - \widetilde{\lambda}_i) = -w_j^T E \widetilde{u}_i.$$

Now let's bound the terms in this expression. First, for any $i \neq j$, we have $|\lambda_j - \widetilde{\lambda}_i| \geq |\lambda_j - \lambda_i| - R \geq \delta - R$ using Gershgorin's disk theorem. Second, $\widetilde{u}_i$ is a unit vector by assumption and $\|w_j\| \leq 1/\sigma_{min}(U)$. Using these bounds and rearranging terms now proves the lemma. ∎

The three lemmas we have proven can be combined to give quantitative bounds on how close U is to $\widetilde{U}$, which was our goal at the outset.

Theorem 3.4.6 *Let M be an $n \times n$ matrix with eigendecomposition $M = UDU^{-1}$. Let $\widetilde{M} = M + E$. Finally, let*

$$\delta = \min_{i \neq j} |D_{i,i} - D_{j,j}|$$

i.e., the minimum separation of eigenvalues of M.

(1) If $\kappa(U)\|E\|n < \frac{\delta}{2}$, then $\widetilde{M}$ is diagonalizable.
(2) Moreover, if $\widetilde{M} = \widetilde{U}\widetilde{D}\widetilde{U}^{-1}$, then there is a permutation $\pi : [n] \to [n]$
   such that for all i

$$\|u_i - \widetilde{u}_{\pi(i)}\| \leq \frac{2\|E\|n}{\sigma_{min}(U)(\delta - \kappa(U)\|E\|n)}$$

where $\{u_i\}_i$ are the columns of U and $\{\widetilde{u}_i\}_i$ are the columns of $\widetilde{U}$.

Proof: The first part of the theorem follows by combining Lemma 3.4.3 and Lemma 3.4.4. For the second part of the theorem, let's fix i and let P be the projection onto the orthogonal complement of u_i. Then, using elementary geometry and the fact that the eigenvectors are all unit vectors, we have

$$\|u_i - \widetilde{u}_{\pi(i)}\| \le 2\|P\widetilde{u}_{\pi(i)}\|.$$

Moreover, we can bound the right-hand side as

$$\|P\widetilde{u}_{\pi(i)}\| = \left\| \sum_{j \ne i} c_j P u_j \right\| \le \sum_{j \ne i} |c_j|.$$

Lemma 3.4.5 supplies the bounds on the coefficients c_j, which completes the proof of the theorem. ∎

You were warned early on that the bound would be messy! It is also by no means optimized. But what you should instead take away is the qualitative corollary that we were after: If $\|E\| \le \text{poly}(1/n, \sigma_{min}(U), 1/\sigma_{max}(U), \delta)$ (i.e., if the sampling noise is small enough compared to the dimensions of the matrix, the condition number of U, and the minimum separation), then U and $\widetilde{U}$ are close.

Back to Tensor Decompositions

Now let's return to Jennrich's algorithm. We've stated enough messy bounds for my taste. So let's cheat from here on out and hide messy bounds using the following notation: Let

$$A \xrightarrow{E \to 0} B$$

signify that as E goes to zero, A converges to B at an inverse polynomial rate. We're going to use this notation as a placeholder. Every time you see it, you should think that you could do the algebra to figure out how close A is to B in terms of E and various other factors we'll collect along the way.

With this notation in hand, what we want to do is *qualitatively* track how the error propagates in Jennrich's algorithm. If we let $\widetilde{T} = T + E$, then $\widetilde{T} \xrightarrow{E \to 0} T$ and $\widetilde{T}^{(a)} \xrightarrow{E \to 0} T^{(a)}$ where $\widetilde{T}^{(a)} = \sum_i a_i \widetilde{T}_{\cdot,\cdot,i}$. We leave it as an exercise for the reader to check that there are natural conditions where

$$(\widetilde{T}^{(b)})^+ \xrightarrow{E \to 0} (T^{(b)})^+.$$

As a hint, this convergence depends on the smallest singular value of $T^{(b)}$. Or, to put it another way, if E is not small compared to the smallest singular value of $T^{(b)}$, then in general we cannot say that $(T^{(b)})^+$ and $(\widetilde{T}^{(b)})^+$ are close.

In any case, combining these facts, we have that

$$\widetilde{T}^{(a)}(\widetilde{T}^{(b)})^+ \xrightarrow{E \to 0} T^{(a)}(T^{(b)})^+.$$

Now we are in good shape. The eigenvectors of the right-hand side are the columns of U. Let the columns of $\widetilde{U}$ be the eigenvectors of the left-hand side. Since the left-hand side is converging to the right-hand side at an inverse polynomial rate, we can invoke our perturbation bounds on eigendecompositions (Theorem 3.4.6) to conclude that their eigenvectors are also converging at an inverse polynomial rate. In particular, $\widetilde{U} \xrightarrow{E \to 0} U$ where we have abused notation, because the convergence above is only after we have applied the appropriate permutation to the columns of $\widetilde{U}$. Similarly, we have $\widetilde{V} \xrightarrow{E \to 0} V$.

Finally, we compute $\widetilde{W}$ by solving a linear system in $\widetilde{U}$ and $\widetilde{V}$. It can be shown that $\widetilde{W} \xrightarrow{E \to 0} W$ using the fact that $\widetilde{U}$ and $\widetilde{V}$ are close to well-conditioned matrices U and V, which means that the linear system we get from taking the tensor product of the ith column in $\widetilde{U}$ with the ith column in $\widetilde{V}$ is also well-conditioned.

These are the full, gory details of how you can prove that Jennrich's algorithm behaves well in the presence of noise. If we make our life easy and in what follows analyze our learning algorithms in the no-noise case ($E = 0$), we can always appeal to various perturbation bounds for eigendecompositions and track through how all the errors propagate to bound how close the factors we find are to the true hidden factors. This is what I meant by good medicine. You don't need to think about these perturbation bounds every time you use tensor decompositions, but you should know that they exist, because they really are what justifies using tensor decompositions for learning problems where there is always sampling noise.

3.5 Exercises

Problem 3-1:

(a) Suppose we want to solve the linear system $Ax = b$ (where $A \in \mathbb{R}^{n \times n}$ is square and invertible) but we are only given access to a noisy vector $\tilde{b}$ satisfying

$$\frac{\|b - \tilde{b}\|}{\|b\|} \leq \varepsilon$$

and a noisy matrix $\tilde{A}$ satisfying $\|A - \tilde{A}\| \leq \delta$ (in operator norm). Let $\tilde{x}$ be the solution to $\tilde{A}\tilde{x} = \tilde{b}$. Show that

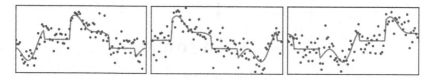

Figure 3.1: Three shifted copies of the true signal x are shown in gray. Noisy samples y_i are shown in red. (Figure credit: [23].)

$$\frac{\|x - \tilde{x}\|}{\|x\|} \leq \frac{\varepsilon \, \sigma_{\max}(A) + \delta}{\sigma_{\min}(A) - \delta}$$

provided $\delta < \sigma_{\min}(A)$.

(b) Now suppose we know A exactly, but A may be badly conditioned or even singular. We want to show that it may still be possible to recover a specific coordinate x_j of x. Let $\tilde{x}$ be any solution to $A\tilde{x} = \tilde{b}$ and let a_i denote column i of A. Show that

$$|x_j - \tilde{x}_j| \leq \frac{\|b - \tilde{b}\|}{C_j}$$

where C_j is the norm of the projection of a_j onto the orthogonal complement of span $(\{a_i\}_{i \neq j})$.

Problem 3-2: In the *multireference alignment* problem, we observe many noisy copies of the same unknown signal $x \in \mathbb{R}^d$, but each copy has been circularly shifted by a random offset (Figure 3.1).

Formally, for $i = 1, 2, \ldots, n$ we observe

$$y_i = R_{\ell_i} x + \xi_i$$

where the ℓ_i are drawn uniformly and independently from $\{0, 1, \ldots, d-1\}$; R_ℓ is the operator that circularly shifts a vector by ℓ indices; $\xi_i \sim \mathcal{N}(0, \sigma^2 I_{d \times d})$ with $\{\xi_i\}_i$ is independent; and $\sigma > 0$ is a known constant. Think of d, x, and σ as fixed while $n \to \infty$. The goal is to recover x (or a circular shift of x).

(a) Consider the tensor $T(x) = \frac{1}{d} \sum_{\ell=0}^{d-1} (R_\ell x) \otimes (R_\ell x) \otimes (R_\ell x)$. Show how to use the samples y_i to estimate T (with error tending to zero as $n \to \infty$). Take extra care with the entries that have repeated indices (e.g., T_{aab}, T_{aaa}).

(b) Given $T(x)$, prove that Jennrich's algorithm can be used to recover x (up to circular shift). Assume that x is *generic* in the following sense: Let $x' \in \mathbb{R}^d$ be arbitrary and let x be obtained from x' by adding a small perturbation $\delta \sim \mathcal{N}(0, \epsilon)$ to the first entry. *Hint:* Form a matrix with rows $\{R_\ell x\}_{0 \leq \ell < d}$, arranged so that the diagonal entries are all x_1.

4

Tensor Decompositions

Applications

Many exciting problems fit into the following paradigm: First, we choose some parametric family of distributions that are rich enough to model things like evolution, writing, and the formation of social networks. Second, we design algorithms for learning the unknown parameters — which you should think of as a proxy for finding hidden structure in our data, like a tree of life that explains how species evolved from each other, the topics that underly a collection of documents, or the communities of strongly connected individuals in a social network. In this chapter, all of our algorithms will be based on tensor decomposition. We will construct a tensor from the moments of our distribution and apply Jennrich's algorithm to find the hidden factors, which in turn will reveal the unknown parameters of our model.

4.1 Phylogenetic Trees and HMMs

Our first application of tensor decomposition is to learning phylogenetic trees. Before we go into the details of the model, it is helpful to understand the motivation. A central problem in evolutionary biology is piecing together the *tree of life*, which describes how species evolved from each other. More precisely, it is a binary tree whose leaves represent *extant* species (i.e., species that are currently living) and whose internal nodes represent *extinct* species. When an internal node has two children, it represents a speciation event, where two populations split off into separate species.

We will work with a stochastic model defined on this tree where each edge introduces its own randomness that represents mutation. More precisely, our model has the following components:

(a) A rooted binary tree with root r (the leaves do not necessarily have the same depth).
(b) A set Σ of states, for example $\Sigma = \{A, C, G, T\}$. Let $k = |\Sigma|$.
(c) A Markov model on the tree; i.e., a distribution π_r on the state of the root and a transition matrix P^{uv} for each edge (u, v).

We can generate a sample from the model as follows: We choose a state for the root according to π_r, and for each node v with parent u we choose the state of v according to the distribution defined by the ith row of P^{uv}, where i is the state of u. Alternatively, we can think of $s(\cdot) : V \to \Sigma$ as a random function that assigns states to vertices where the marginal distribution on $s(r)$ is π_r and

$$P^{uv}_{ij} = \mathbb{P}(s(v) = j | s(u) = i).$$

Note that $s(v)$ is independent of $s(t)$ conditioned on $s(u)$ whenever the (unique) shortest path from v to t in the tree passes through u.

In this section, our main goal is to learn the rooted tree and the transition matrices when given enough samples from the model. Now is a good time to connect this back to biology. What does a sample from this model represent? If we have sequenced each of the extant species and, moreover, these sequences have already been properly aligned, we can think of the ith symbol in each of these sequences as being represented by the configuration of the states of the leaves in a sample from the above model. Of course this is an oversimplification of the biological problem, but it still captures many interesting phenomena.

There are really two separate tasks: (a) learning the topology and (b) estimating the transition matrices. Our approach for finding the topology will follow the foundational work of Steel [133] and Erdos, Steel, Szekely, and Warnow [69]. Once we know the topology, we can apply tensor decompositions to find the transition matrices following the approach of Chang [47] and Mossel and Roch [115].

Learning the Topology

Here we will focus on the problem of learning the topology of the tree. The amazing idea credited to Steel [133] is that there is a way to define an *evolutionary distance*. What is important about this distance is that it (a) assigns a nonnegative value to every edge in the tree and (b) can be evaluated for any pair of nodes given just their joint distribution. So what magical function has these properties? First, for any pair of nodes a and b, let F^{ab} be a $k \times k$ matrix that represents their joint distribution:

$$F^{ab}_{ij} = \mathbb{P}(s(a) = i, s(b) = j).$$

Definition 4.1.1 *Steel's evolutionary distance on an edge* (u, v) *is*

$$v_{uv} = -\ln |det(P^{uv})| + \frac{1}{2} \ln \left(\prod_{i \in [k]} \pi_u(i) \right) - \frac{1}{2} \ln \left(\prod_{i \in [k]} \pi_v(i) \right).$$

Steel [133] proved two fundamental properties of this distance function, captured in the following lemma:

Lemma 4.1.2 *Steel's evolutionary distance satisfies:*

(a) v_{uv} *is nonnegative and*
(b) for any pair of nodes a and b, we have

$$\psi_{ab} := -\ln |det(F^{ab})| = \sum_{(u,v) \in p_{ab}} v_{uv}$$

where p_{ab} *is the shortest path connecting a and b in the tree.*

What makes this distance so useful for our purposes is that for any pair of leaves a and b, we can estimate F^{ab} from our samples, and hence we can (approximately) compute ψ_{ab} on the leaves. So from now on, we can imagine that there is some nonnegative function on the edges of the tree and that we have an oracle for computing the sum of the distances along the path connecting any two leaves.

Reconstructing Quartets

Now we will use Steel's evolutionary distance to compute the topology by piecing together the picture four nodes at a time.

Our goal is to determine which of these induced topologies is the true topology, given the pairwise distances.

Lemma 4.1.3 *If all distances in the tree are strictly positive, then it is possible to determine the induced topology on any four nodes a, b, c, and d given an oracle that can compute the distance between any pair of them.*

Proof: The proof is by case analysis. Consider the three possible induced topologies between the nodes a, b, c, and d, as depicted in Figure 4.1. Here by induced topology, we mean delete edges not on any shortest path between any pair of the four leaves and contract paths to a single edge if possible.

It is easy to check that under topology (a) we have

$$\psi(a, b) + \psi(c, d) < \min \{\psi(a, c) + \psi(b, c), \psi(a, d) + \psi(b, d)\}.$$

But under topology (b) or (c) this inequality would not hold. There is an analogous way to identify each of the other topologies, again based on the

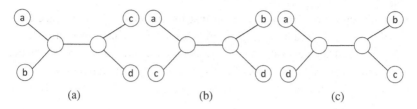

Figure 4.1: Possible quartet topologies

pairwise distances. What this means is that we can simply compute three values: $\psi(a,b) + \psi(c,d)$, $\psi(a,c) + \psi(b,c)$, and $\psi(a,d) + \psi(b,d)$. Whichever is the smallest determines the induced topology as being (a), (b), or (c), respectively. ∎

Indeed, from just these quartet tests, we can recover the topology of the tree.

Lemma 4.1.4 *If for any quadruple of leaves a, b, c, and d we can determine the induced topology, it is possible to determine the topology of the tree.*

Proof: The approach is to first determine which pairs of leaves have the same parent, and then determine which pairs have the same grandparent, and so on. First, fix a pair of leaves a and b. It is easy to see that they have the same parent if and only if for every other choice of leaves c and d, the quartet test returns topology (a). Now, if we want to determine whether a pair of leaves a and b have the same grandparent, we can modify the approach as follows: They have the same grandparent if and only if for every other choice of leaves c and d, neither of which is a sibling of a or b, the quartet test returns topology (a). Essentially, we are building up the tree by finding the closest pairs first. ∎

An important technical point is that we can only approximate F^{ab} from our samples. This translates into a good approximation of ψ_{ab} when a and b are close, but is noisy when a and b are far away. Ultimately, the approach in [69] of Erdos, Steel, Szekely, and Warnow is to use quartet tests only where all the distances are short.

Estimating the Transition Matrices

Now we will assume that we know the topology of the tree and set our sights on estimating the transition matrices. Our approach is to use tensor decompositions. To that end, for any triple of leaves a, b, and c, let T^{abc} be the $k \times k \times k$ tensor, defined as follows:

$$T^{abc}_{ijk} = \mathbb{P}(s(a) = i, s(b) = j, s(c) = k).$$

These are third-order moments of our distribution that we can estimate from samples. We will assume throughout this section that the transition matrices are full rank. This means that we can reroot the tree arbitrarily. Now consider the unique node that lies on all of the shortest paths among a, b, and c. Let's let this be the root. Then

$$T^{abc} = \sum_{\ell} \mathbb{P}(s(r) = \ell)\mathbb{P}(s(a) = \cdot|s(r) = \ell) \otimes \mathbb{P}(s(b) = \cdot|s(r) = \ell)$$

$$\otimes \mathbb{P}(s(c) = \cdot|s(r) = \ell)$$

$$= \sum_{\ell} \mathbb{P}(s(r) = \ell)P^{ra}_{\ell} \otimes P^{rb}_{\ell} \otimes P^{rc}_{\ell}$$

where we have used P^{rx}_{ℓ} to denote the ℓth row of the transition matrix P^{rx}.

We can now apply the algorithm in Section 3.3 to compute a tensor decomposition of T whose factors are unique up to rescaling. Furthermore, the factors are probability distributions and hence we can compute their proper normalization. We will call this procedure a *star test*. (Indeed, the algorithm for tensor decompositions in Section 3.3 has been rediscovered many times, and it is also called Chang's lemma [47].)

In [115], Mossel and Roch used this approach to find the transition matrices of a phylogenetic tree given the tree topology, as follows. Let us assume that u and v are internal nodes and that w is a leaf. Furthermore, suppose that v lies on the shortest path between u and w. The basic idea is to write

$$P^{uw} = P^{uv}P^{vw}$$

and if we can find P^{uw} and P^{vw} (using the star tests above), then we can compute $P^{uv} = P^{uw}(P^{vw})^{-1}$ since we have assumed that the transition matrices are invertible.

However, there are two serious complications:

(a) As in the case of finding the topology, long paths are very noisy.

Mossel and Roch showed that one can recover the transition matrices also using only queries to short paths.

(b) We can only recover the tensor decomposition up to relabeling.

In the above star test, we could apply any permutation to the states of r and permute the rows of the transition matrices P^{ra}, P^{rb}, and P^{rc} accordingly so that the resulting joint distribution on a, b, and c is unchanged.

However, the approach of Mossel and Roch is to work instead in the *probably approximately correct* learning framework of Valiant [138], where the goal is to learn a generative model that produces almost the same joint distribution on the leaves. In particular, if there are multiple ways to label the internal nodes to produce the same joint distribution on the leaves, we are indifferent to them.

Remark 4.1.5 *Hidden Markov models are a special case of phylogenetic trees, where the underlying topology is a caterpillar. But note that for the above algorithm, we need that the transition matrices* and *the observation matrices are full rank.*

More precisely, we require that the transition matrices are invertible and that the observation matrices, with the convention that the rows are indexed by the states of the corresponding hidden node and whose columns are indexed by the output symbols each have full row rank.

Beyond Full Rank?

The algorithm above assumes that all transition matrices are full rank. In fact, if we remove this assumption, then it is easy to embed an instance of the *noisy parity problem* [37], which is a classic hard learning problem. Let us first define this problem *without noise*:

Let $S \subset [n]$, and choose $X^{(j)} \in \{0,1\}^n$ independently and uniformly at random for $j = 1, \ldots, m$. Given $X^{(j)}$ and $b^{(j)} = \chi_S(X^{(j)}) := \sum_{i \in S} X_i^{(j)} \mod 2$ for each j, the goal is to recover S.

This is quite easy: Let A be the matrix whose j^{th} row is $X^{(j)}$ and let b be a column vector whose j^{th} entry is $b^{(j)}$. It is straightforward to see that $\mathbb{1}_S$ is a solution to the linear system $Ax = b$ where $\mathbb{1}_S$ is the indicator function for S. Furthermore, if we choose $\Omega(n \log n)$ samples, then A is with high probability full column rank, and so this solution is unique. We can then find S by solving a linear system over $GF(2)$.

Yet a slight change in the above problem does not change the sample complexity, but makes the problem drastically harder. The noisy parity problem is the same as above, but for each j we are independently given the value $b^{(j)} = \chi_S(X^{(j)})$ with probability 2/3 and otherwise $b^{(j)} = 1 - \chi_S(X_j)$. The challenge is that we do not know which labels have been flipped.

Claim 4.1.6 *There is an exponential time algorithm that solves the noisy parity problem using $m = O(n \log n)$ samples.*

Proof: For each T, calculate the fraction of samples where χ_T agrees with the observed label — i.e.,

$$\frac{1}{m} \sum_{j=1}^{m} \mathbb{1}_{\chi_T(X^{(j)})=b^{(j)}}.$$

From standard concentration bounds, it follows that with high probability this value is larger than (say) $3/5$ if and only if $S = T$. ∎

The best-known algorithm due to Blum, Kalai, and Wasserman [37] has running time and sample complexity $2^{n/\log n}$. It is widely believed that there is no polynomial time algorithm for noisy parity even given any polynomial number of samples. *This is an excellent example of a problem whose sample complexity and computational complexity are (conjectured to be) wildly different.*

Next we show how to embed samples from a noisy parity problem into an HMM; however, to do so, we will make use of transition matrices that are not full rank. Consider an HMM that has n hidden nodes, where the ith hidden node encoded is used to represent the ith coordinate of X, and the running parity

$$\chi_{S_i}(X) := \sum_{i' \leq i, i' \in S} X(i') \quad \text{mod } 2.$$

Hence each node has four possible states. We can define the following transition matrices. Let $s(i) = (x_i, s_i)$ be the state of the ith internal node, where $s_i = \chi_{S_i}(X)$.

We can define the following transition matrices:

$$\text{if } i+1 \in S \qquad P^{i,i+1} = \begin{cases} \frac{1}{2} & (0, s_i) \\ \frac{1}{2} & (1, s_i + 1 \quad \text{mod } 2) \\ 0 & \text{otherwise} \end{cases}$$

$$\text{if } i+1 \notin S \qquad P^{i,i+1} = \begin{cases} \frac{1}{2} & (0, s_i) \\ \frac{1}{2} & (1, s_i) \\ 0 & \text{otherwise} \end{cases} \cdot$$

At each internal node we observe x_i, and at the last node we also observe $\chi_S(X)$ with probability $2/3$ and otherwise $1 - \chi_S(X)$. Each sample from the noisy parity problem is a set of observations from this HMM, and if we could learn its transition matrices, we would necessarily learn S and solve the noisy parity problem.

Note that here the observation matrices are certainly not full rank, because we only observe two possible emissions even though each internal node has four possible states! Hence these problems become much harder when the transition (or observation) matrices are not full rank!

4.2 Community Detection

Here we give applications of tensor methods to community detection. There are many settings in which we would like to discover *communities* — that is, groups of strongly connected individuals. Here we will focus on graph theoretic approaches, where we will think of a community as a set of nodes that are better connected to each other than to nodes outside of the set. There are many ways we could formalize this notion, each of which would lead to a different optimization problem, e.g., *sparsest cut* or *k-densest subgaph*.

However, each of these optimization problems is *NP*-hard and, even worse, is hard to approximate. Instead, we will formulate our problem in an average-case model where there is an underlying community structure that is used to generate a random graph, and our goal is to recover the true communities from the graph with high probability.

Stochastic Block Model

Here we introduce the stochastic block model, which is used to generate a random graph on V with $|V| = n$. Additionally, the model is specified by parameters p and q and a partitioning specified by a function π:

- $\pi : V \to [k]$ partitions the vertices V into k *disjoint* groups (we will relax this condition later).
- Each possible edge (u, v) is chosen *independently* with

$$\mathbb{P}[(u, v) \in E] = \begin{cases} q & \pi(u) = \pi(v) \\ p & \text{otherwise} \end{cases}.$$

In our setting we will set $q > p$, which is called the *assortative* case, but this model also makes sense when $q < p$, which is called the *disassortative* case. For example, when $q = 0$, we are generating a random graph that has a planted k-coloring. Regardless, we observe a random graph generated from the above model and our goal is to recover the partition described by π.

When is this *information theoretically* possible? In fact, even for $k = 2$, where π is a bisection, we need

$$q - p > \Omega\left(\sqrt{\frac{\log n}{n}}\right)$$

in order for the true bisection to be the uniquely smallest cut that bisects the random graph G with high probability. If $q - p$ is smaller, then it is not even information theoretically possible to find π. Indeed, we should also require that each part of the partition is large, and for simplicity we will assume that $k = O(1)$ and $|\{u|\pi(u) = i\}| = \Omega(n)$.

There has been a long line of work on partitioning random graphs in the stochastic block model, culminating in the work of McSherry [109]:

Theorem 4.2.1 *[109] There is an efficient algorithm that recovers π (up to relabeling) if*

$$\frac{q-p}{q} > c\sqrt{\frac{\log n/\delta}{qn}}$$

and succeeds with probability at least $1 - \delta$.

This algorithm is based on spectral clustering, where we think of the observed adjacency matrix as the sum of a rank k matrix that encodes π and an error term. If the error is small, then we can recover something close to the true rank k matrix by finding the best rank k approximation to the adjacency matrix. For full details, see [109].

We will instead follow the approach in Anandkumar et al. [9] that makes use of tensor decompositions. In fact, their algorithm also works in the *mixed membership* model, where we allow each node to be a distribution over $[k]$. Then, if π^u and π^v are the probability distributions for u and v, the probability of an edge (u, v) is $\sum_i \pi_i^u \pi_i^v q + \sum_{i \neq j} \pi_i^u \pi_j^v p$. We can interpret this probability as: u and v choose a community according to π^u and π^v, respectively, and if they choose the same community, there is an edge with probability q, and otherwise there is an edge with probability p.

Counting Three Stars

What's really going on when we use tensor decompositions is that we are finding conditionally independent random variables. That's what we did when we used them for learning the transition matrices of a phylogenetic tree. There, the states of a, b, and c were independent once we conditioned on the state of the unique node r where the shortest paths between them met. We will do something similar here.

If we have four nodes a, b, c, and x and we condition on which community x belongs to, then whether or not (a, x), (b, x), and (c, x) are edges in our graph they are are all independent random variables. When all three edges are present, this is called a *three star*. We will set up a tensor that counts three stars as follows. First we partition V into four sets X, A, B, and C. Now let $\Pi \in \{0, 1\}^{V \times k}$ represent the (unknown) assignment of nodes to communities, so that each row of Π contains exactly one 1. Finally, let R be the $k \times k$ matrix whose entries are the connection probabilities. In particular,

$$(R)_{ij} = \begin{cases} q & i = j \\ p & i \neq j \end{cases}.$$

Consider the product ΠR. The ith column of ΠR encodes the probability that there is an edge from a node in community i to the node corresponding to the given row.

$$(\Pi R)_{xi} = \Pr[(x, a) \in E | \pi(a) = i].$$

We will use $(\Pi R)_i^A$ to denote the matrix ΠR restricted to the ith column and the rows in A, and similarly for B and C. Moreover, let p_i be the fraction of nodes in X that are in community i. Then our algorithm revolves around the following tensor:

$$T = \sum_i p_i (\Pi R)_i^A \otimes (\Pi R)_i^B \otimes (\Pi R)_i^C.$$

The key claim is:

Claim 4.2.2 *Let $a \in A$, $b \in B$ and $c \in C$, then*

$$T_{a,b,c} = \mathbb{P}[(x, a), (x, b), (x, c) \in E]$$

where the randomness is over x chosen uniformly at random from X and the edges included in G.

This is immediate from the discussion above. With this tensor in hand, the key things we need to prove are:

(a) The factors $\{(\Pi R)_i^A\}_i$, $\{(\Pi R)_i^B\}_i$, and $\{(\Pi R)_i^B\}_i$ are linearly independent.
(b) We can recover the partition π from $\{(\Pi R)_i^A\}_i$ up to relabeling which community is which.

We will ignore the problem of estimating T accurately, but roughly this amounts to choosing X to be much larger than A, B, or C and applying the appropriate concentration bounds. In any case, let's now figure out why the hidden factors are linearly independent.

Lemma 4.2.3 *If A, B, and C have at least one node from each community, then the factors $\{(\Pi R)_i^A\}_i$, $\{(\Pi R)_i^B\}_i$, and $\{(\Pi R)_i^B\}_i$ are each linearly independent.*

Proof: First, it is easy to see that R is full rank. Now, if A has at least one node from each community, each row of R appears in $(\Pi R)^A$, which means that it has full column rank. An identical argument works for B and C too. ∎

Actually, we need the factors to be not just full rank, but also well conditioned. The same type of argument as in the previous lemma shows that as long as each community is well represented in A, B, and C (which happens with high probability if A, B, and C are large enough and chosen at random), then the factors $\{(\Pi R)_i^A\}_i$, $\{(\Pi R)_i^B\}_i$, and $\{(\Pi R)_i^B\}_i$ will be well conditioned.

Now let's recover the community structure from the hidden factors: First, if we have $\{(\Pi R)_i^A\}_i$, then we can partition A into communities just by grouping together nodes whose corresponding rows are the same. In turn, if A is large enough, then we can extend this partitioning to the whole graph: We add a node $x \notin A$ to community i if and only if the fraction of nodes $a \in A$ with $\pi(a) = i$ that x is connected to is close to q. If A is large enough and we have recovered its community structure correctly, then with high probability this procedure will recover the true communities in the entire graph.

For a full analysis of the algorithm, including its sample complexity and accuracy, see [9]. Anandkumar et al. also give an algorithm for mixed membership models, where each π_u is chosen from a Dirichlet distribution. We will not cover this latter extension, because we will instead explain those types of techniques in the setting of topic models next.

Discussion

We note that there are powerful extensions to the stochastic block model that are called *semirandom models*. Roughly, these models allow a *monotone adversary* to add edges between nodes in the same cluster and delete edges between clusters after G is generated. It sounds like the adversary is only making your life easier by strengthening ties within a community and breaking ties across them. If the true community structure is the partition of G into k parts that cuts the fewest edges, then this is only more true after the changes. Interestingly, many tensor and spectral algorithms break down in the semirandom model, but there are elegant techniques for recovering π even in this more general setting (see [71], [72]). *This is some food for thought and begs the question: How much are we exploiting brittle properties of our stochastic model?*

4.3 Extensions to Mixed Models

Many of the models we have studied so far can be generalized to so-called *mixed membership models*. For example, instead of a document being about just one topic, we can model it as a mixture of topics. And instead of an individual belonging to just one community, we can model her as belonging to a mixture of communities. Here we will leverage tensor decompositions in mixed membership settings.

Pure Topic Model

As a warm-up, let's first see how tensor decompositions can be used to discover the topics of a pure topic model where every document is about just one topic. Our approach will follow that of Anandkumar et al. [10]. Recall that in a pure topic model, there is an unknown $m \times r$ topic matrix A and each document is generated according to the following stochastic process:

(a) Choose topic i for document j with probability p_i.
(b) Choose N_j words according to the distribution A_i.

In Section 2.4 we constructed the Gram matrix, which represents the joint distribution of pairs of words. Here we will use the joint distribution of triples of words. Let w_1, w_2, and w_3 denote the random variables for its first, second, and third words, respectively.

Definition 4.3.1 *Let T denote the $m \times m \times m$ tensor where*

$$T_{a,b,c} = \mathbb{P}[w_1 = a, w_2 = b, w_3 = c].$$

We can express T in terms of the unknown topic matrix as follows:

$$T = \sum_{i=1}^{r} p_i A_i \otimes A_i \otimes A_i$$

So how can we recover the topic matrix given samples from a pure topic model? We can construct an estimated $\widetilde{T}$ where $\widetilde{T}_{a,b,c}$ counts the fraction of documents in our sample whose first word, second word and third word, are a, b, and c, respectively. If the number of documents is large enough, then $\widetilde{T}$ converges to T.

Now we can apply Jennrich's algorithm. Provided that A has full column rank, we will recover the true factors in the decomposition up to a rescaling. However, since each column in A is a distribution, we can properly normalize whatever hidden factors we find and compute the values of p_i too. To really make this work, we need to analyze how many documents we need in order for $\widetilde{T}$ to be close to T, and then apply the results in Section 3.4, where we analyzed the noise tolerance of Jennrich's algorithm. The important point is that the columns of our estimated $\widetilde{A}$ converge to columns of A at an inverse polynomial rate with the number of samples we are given, where the rate of convergence depends on things like how well conditioned the columns of A are.

Latent Dirichlet Allocation

Now let's move on to mixed membership models. What has driven all the applications of tensor decomposition we've seen so far have been conditionally independent random variables. In the case of pure topic models, the distributions of the first three words is independent when we condition on the topic that is being used to generate the document. However, in mixed models it will not be so simple. The way we construct a low-rank third-order tensor from the data that we have available to us will combine lower-order statistics in more complicated ways.

We will study the latent Dirichlet allocation model, which was introduced in the seminal work of Blei et al. [36]. Let $\Delta := \{x \in \mathbb{R}^r : x \geq 0, \sum_i x_i = 1\}$ denote the r-dimensional simplex. Then each document is generated according to the following stochastic process:

(a) Choose a mixture over topics $w_j \in \Delta$ for document j according to the Dirichlet distribution $\text{Dir}(\{\alpha_i\}_i)$.
(b) Repeat N_j times: choose a topic i from w_j, and choose a word according to the distribution A_i.

And the Dirichlet distribution is defined as

$$p(x) \propto \prod_i x_i^{\alpha_i - 1} \text{ for } x \in \Delta.$$

This model is already more realistic in the following way. When documents are long (say $N_j > m \log m$), then in a pure topic model, pairs of documents would necessarily have nearly identical empirical distributions on words. But this is no longer the case in mixed models like the one above.

The basic issue in extending our tensor decomposition approach for learning pure topic models to mixed models is that the third-order tensor that counts the joint distribution of triples of words now satisfies the following expression:

$$T = \sum_{ijk} D_{ijk} A_i \otimes A_j \otimes A_k$$

where $D_{i,j,k}$ is the probability that the first three words in a random document are generated from topics i, j, and k, respectively. In a pure topic model, $D_{i,j,k}$ is diagonal, but for a mixed model it is not!

Definition 4.3.2 *A Tucker decomposition of T is*

$$T = \sum_{i,j,k} D_{i,j,k} a_i \otimes b_j \otimes c_k$$

where D is $r_1 \times r_2 \times r_3$. We call D the core tensor.

It turns out that you can compute a Tucker decomposition where r_1, r_2, and r_3 are as small as possible (they turn out to be the dimensions of the span of the columns, rows, and tubes, respectively). However, a minimal Tucker decomposition, is usually not unique, so even if we are given T and we compute a minimal Tucker decomposition we have no guarantee that its factors are the hidden topics in the topic model. We will need to find another way, which amounts to constructing a low-rank third-order tensor out of T and lower-order moments we have access to as well.

So how can we extend the tensor decomposition approach to work for latent Dirichlet allocation models? The elegant approach of Anandkumar et al. [8] is based on the following idea:

Lemma 4.3.3

$$T = \sum_{ijk} D_{ijk} A_i \otimes A_j \otimes A_k$$

$$S = \sum_{ijk} \widetilde{D}_{ijk} A_i \otimes A_j \otimes A_k$$

$$\implies T - S = \sum_{ijk} (D_{ijk} - \widetilde{D}_{ijk}) A_i \otimes A_j \otimes A_k$$

Proof: The proof is a simple exercise in multilinear algebra. ∎

Hence, if we have access to other tensors S that can be written using the same factors $\{A_i\}_i$ in their Tucker decompositions, we can subtract T and S and hope to make the core tensor diagonal. We can think of D as being the third-order moment of a Dirichlet distribution in our setting. What other tensors do we have access to?

Other Tensors

We described the tensor T based on the following experiment: Let $T_{a,b,c}$ be the probability that the first three words in a random document are a, b, and c, respectively. But we could just as well consider alternative experiments. The two other experiments we will need in order to given a tensor spectral algorithm for LDA are:

(a) Choose three documents at random, and look at the first word of each document.
(b) Choose two documents at random, and look at the first two words of the first document and the first word of the second document.

These two new experiments combined with the old experiment result in three tensors whose Tucker decompositions use the same factors but whose core tensors differ.

Definition 4.3.4 *Let μ, M, and D be the first-, second-, and third-order moments of the Dirichlet distribution.*

More precisely, let μ_i be the probability that the first word in a random document is generated from topic i. Let $M_{i,j}$ be the probability that the first and second words in a random document are generated from topics i and j, respectively. And as before, let $D_{i,j,k}$ be the probability that the first three words in a random document are generated from topics i, j, and k, respectively. Then let T^1, T^2, and T^3 be the expectations of the first (choose three documents), second (choose two documents), and third (choose one document) experiment, respectively.

Lemma 4.3.5 *(a)* $T^1 = \sum_{i,j,k} [\mu \otimes \mu \otimes \mu]_{i,j,k} A_i \otimes A_j \otimes A_k$
(b) $T^2 = \sum_{i,j,k} [M \otimes \mu]_{i,j,k} A_i \otimes A_j \otimes A_k$
(c) $T^3 = \sum_{i,j,k} D_{i,j,k} A_i \otimes A_j \otimes A_k$

Proof: Let w_1 denote the first word and let t_1 denote the topic of w_1 (and similarly for the other words). We can expand $\mathbb{P}[w_1 = a, w_2 = b, w_3 = c]$ as:

$$\sum_{i,j,k} \mathbb{P}[w_1 = a, w_2 = b, w_3 = c | t_1 = i, t_2 = j, t_3 = k] \mathbb{P}[t_1 = i, t_2 = j, t_3 = k]$$

and the lemma is now immediate. ∎

Note that $T^2_{a,b,c} \neq T^2_{a,c,b}$ because two of the words come from the same document. Nevertheless, we can symmetrize T^2 in the natural way: Set $S^2_{a,b,c} = T^2_{a,b,c} + T^2_{b,c,a} + T^2_{c,a,b}$. Hence $S^2_{a,b,c} = S^2_{\pi(a),\pi(b),\pi(c)}$ for any permutation $\pi : \{a, b, c\} \to \{a, b, c\}$.

Our main goal is to prove the following identity:

$$\alpha_0^2 D + 2(\alpha_0 + 1)(\alpha_0 + 2)\mu^{\otimes 3} - \alpha_0(\alpha_0 + 2)M \otimes \mu \text{(all three ways)} = \text{diag}(\{p_i\}_i)$$

where $\alpha_0 = \sum_i \alpha_i$. Hence we have that

$$\alpha_0^2 T^3 + 2(\alpha_0 + 1)(\alpha_0 + 2)T^1 - \alpha_0(\alpha_0 + 2)S^2 = \sum_i p_i A_i \otimes A_i \otimes A_i.$$

The important point is that we can estimate the terms on the left-hand side from our sample (if we assume we know α_0) and we can apply Jennrich's algorithm to the tensor on the right-hand side to recover the topic model, provided that A has full column rank. In fact, we can compute α_0 from our samples (see [8]), but we will focus instead on proving the above identity.

Moments of the Dirichlet

The main identity that we would like to establish is just a statement about the moments of a Dirichlet distribution. In fact, we can think about the Dirichlet as being defined by the following combinatorial process:

(a) Initially, there are α_i balls of each color i.
(b) Repeat C times: choose a ball at random, place it back with one more of its own color.

This process gives an alternative characterization of the Dirichlet distribution, from which it is straightforward to calculate:

(a) $\mu = [\frac{\alpha_1}{\alpha_0}, \frac{\alpha_2}{\alpha_0}, \ldots, \frac{\alpha_r}{\alpha_0}]$

(b) $M_{i,j} = \begin{cases} \frac{\alpha_i(\alpha_i+1)}{\alpha_0(\alpha_0+1)} & i = j \\ \frac{\alpha_i\alpha_j}{\alpha_0(\alpha_0+1)} & \text{otherwise} \end{cases}$

(c) $T_{i,j,k} = \begin{cases} \frac{\alpha_i(\alpha_i+1)(\alpha_i+2)}{\alpha_0(\alpha_0+1)(\alpha_0+2)} & i = j = k \\ \frac{\alpha_i(\alpha_i+1)\alpha_k}{\alpha_0(\alpha_0+1)(\alpha_0+2)} & i = j \neq k \\ \frac{\alpha_i\alpha_j\alpha_k}{\alpha_0(\alpha_0+1)(\alpha_0+2)} & i, j, k \text{ distinct} \end{cases}$

For example, for $T_{i,i,k}$ this is the probability that the first two balls are color i and the third ball is color k. The probability that the first ball is color i is $\frac{\alpha_i}{\alpha_0}$, and since we place it back with one more of its own color, the probability that the second ball is also color i is $\frac{\alpha_i+1}{\alpha_0+1}$. And the probability that the third ball is color k is $\frac{\alpha_k}{\alpha_0+2}$. It is easy to check the above formulas in the other cases too.

Note that it is much easier to think about only the numerators in the above formulas. If we can prove that following relation for just the numerators

$$D + 2\mu^{\otimes 3} - M \otimes \mu(\text{all three ways}) = \text{diag}(\{2\alpha_i\}_i)$$

it is easy to check that we would obtain our desired formula by multiplying through by $\alpha_0^3(\alpha_0 + 1)(\alpha_0 + 2)$.

Definition 4.3.6 *Let $R = num(D) + num(2\mu^{\otimes 3}) - num(M \otimes \mu)(\text{all three ways})$.*

Then the main lemma is:

Lemma 4.3.7 $R = diag(\{2\alpha_i\}_i)$

We will establish this by a case analysis:

Claim 4.3.8 *If i, j, k are distinct, then $R_{i,j,k} = 0$.*

This is immediate, since the i, j, k numerators of D, $\mu^{\otimes 3}$, and $M \otimes \mu$ are all $\alpha_i \alpha_j \alpha_k$.

Claim 4.3.9 $R_{i,i,i} = 2\alpha_i$

This is also immediate, since the i, i, i numerator of D is $\alpha_i(\alpha_i + 1)(\alpha_i + 2)$ and similarly, the numerator of $\mu^{\otimes 3}$ is α_i^3. Finally, the i, i, i numerator of $M \otimes \mu$ is $\alpha_i^2(\alpha_i + 1)$. The case that requires some care is:

Claim 4.3.10 *If $i \neq k$, $R_{i,i,k} = 0$.*

The reason this case is tricky is because the terms $M \otimes \mu$(all three ways) do not all count the same. If we think of μ along the third dimension of the tensor, then the ith topic occurs twice in the same document, but if instead we think of μ as along either the first or second dimension of the tensor, even though the ith topic occurs twice, it does not occur twice in the same document. Hence the numerator of $M \otimes \mu$(all three ways) is $\alpha_i(\alpha_i + 1)\alpha_k + 2\alpha_i^2\alpha_k$. Also, the numerator of D is $\alpha_i(\alpha_i + 1)\alpha_k$ and the numerator of $\mu^{\otimes 3}$ is again $\alpha_i^2\alpha_k$.

These three claims together establish the above lemma. Even though the tensor T^3 that we could immediately decompose in a pure topic model no longer has a diagonal core tensor in a mixed model, at least in the case of LDA we can still find a formula (each of whose terms we can estimate from our samples) that diagonalizes the core tensor. This yields:

Theorem 4.3.11 *[8] There is a polynomial time algorithm to learn a topic matrix $\widetilde{A}$ whose columns are ϵ-close in Euclidean distance to the columns of A in a latent Dirichlet allocation model, provided we are given at least $poly(m, 1/\epsilon, 1/\sigma_r, 1/\alpha_{min})$ documents of length at least three, where m is the size of the vocabulary and σ_r is the smallest singular value of A and α_{min} is the smallest α_i.*

Epilogue

The algorithm of Anandkumar et al. [9] for learning mixed membership stochastic block models follows the same pattern. Once again, the Dirichlet distribution plays a key role. Instead of each node belonging to just one community, as in the usual stochastic block model, each node is described by a distribution π_u over communities where π_u is chosen from a Dirichlet distribution. The main idea is to count three stars and to add and subtract tensors constructed from lower-order subgraph counts to make the core tensor in the natural Tucker decomposition diagonal.

It is worth mentioning that these techniques seem specialized to Dirichlet distributions. As we have seen, conditionally independent random variables play a key role in tensor decompositions. In mixed membership models, finding such random variables is challenging. But how far is the Dirichlet distribution from being independent? Even though the coordinates are not independent, it turns out that they almost are. You can instead sample from a Dirichlet distribution by sampling from a beta distribution for each coordinate independently and then renormalizing the vector so that it is in the r-dimensional simplex. An interesting conceptual question going forward is: *Are tensor decomposition methods fundamentally limited to settings where there is some sort of independence?*

4.4 Independent Component Analysis

We can think about the tensor methods we have developed as a way to use higher-order moments to learn the parameters of a distribution (e.g., for phylogenetic trees, HMMs, LDA, community detection) through tensor decomposition. Here we will give another style of using the method of moments through an application to *independent component analysis*, which was introduced by Comon [53].

This problem is simple to define: Suppose we are given samples of the form

$$y = Ax + b$$

where we know that the variables x_i are independent and the linear transformation (A, b) is unknown. The goal is to learn A, b efficiently from a polynomial number of samples. This problem has a long history, and the typical motivation for it is to consider a hypothetical situation called the *cocktail party problem*:

> We have n microphones and n conversations going on in a room. Each microphone hears a superposition of the conversations given by the corresponding rows of A. If we think of the conversations as independent and memoryless, can we disentangle them?

Such problems are also often referred to as *blind source separation*. We will follow an approach of Frieze, Jerrum, and Kannan [74]. What's really neat about their approach is that it uses nonconvex optimization.

A Canonical Form and Rotational Invariance

Let's first put our problem into a more convenient canonical form. It turns out we can assume we are given samples from

$$y = Ax + b$$

but where for all i, $E[x_i] = 0, \mathbb{E}[x_i^2] = 1$. The idea is that if any variable x_i were not mean zero, we could make it mean zero and add a correction to b. And similarly, if x_i were not variance one, we could rescale both it and the corresponding column of A to make its variance be one. These changes are just notational and do not affect the distribution on samples that we observe. So from here on out, let's assume that we are given samples in the above canonical form.

We will give an algorithm based on nonconvex optimization for estimating A and b. But first let's discuss what assumptions we will need. We will make two assumptions: (a) A is nonsingular and (b) every variable satisfies $\mathbb{E}[x_i^4] \neq 3$. You should be used to nonsingularity assumptions by now (it's what we need every time we use Jennrich's algorithm). But what about the second assumption? Where does it come from? It turns out that it is actually quite natural and is needed to rule out a problematic case.

Claim 4.4.1 *If each x_i is an independent standard Gaussian, then for any orthogonal transformation R, x and Rx, and consequently*

$$y = Ax + b \text{ and } y = ARx + b$$

have identical distributions.

Proof: The standard n-dimensional Gaussian is rotationally invariant. ∎

What this means is that when our independent random variables are standard Gaussians, it is information theoretically impossible to distinguish between A and AR. Actually the n-dimensional Gaussian is the *only* problematic case. There are other rotationally invariant distributions, such as the uniform distribution on $\mathbb{S}^{n-1}$, but its coordinates are not independent. The standard n-dimensional Gaussian is the only rotationally invariant distribution whose coordinates are independent.

In light of this discussion, we can understand where our assumption about the fourth moments comes from. For a standard Gaussian distribution, its mean is zero, its variance is one, and its fourth moment is three. So our assumption on the fourth moment of each x_i is just a way to say that it is noticeably non-Gaussian.

Whitening

As usual, we cannot hope to learn A from just the second moments. This is really the same issue that arose when we discussed the rotation problem. In the case of tensor decompositions, we went directly to the third-order moment to learn the columns of A through Jennrich's algorithm. Here we will learn what we can from the first and second moments, and then move on to the fourth moment. In particular, we will use the first and second moments to learn b and to learn A up to a rotation:

Lemma 4.4.2 $\mathbb{E}[y] = b$ and $\mathbb{E}[yy^T] = AA^T$

Proof: The first identity is obvious. For the second, we can compute

$$\mathbb{E}[yy^T] = \mathbb{E}[Axx^T A^T] = A\,\mathbb{E}[xx^T]A^T = AA^T$$

where the last equality follows from the condition that $E[x_i] = 0$ and $E[x_i^2] = 1$ and that each x_i is independent. ∎

What this means is that we can estimate b and $M = AA^T$ to arbitrary precision by taking enough samples. What I claim is that this determines A up to a rotation. Since $M \succ 0$, we can find B such that $M = BB^T$ using the Cholesky factorization. But how are B and A related?

Lemma 4.4.3 *There is an orthogonal transformation R so that $BR = A$.*

Proof: Recall that we assumed A is nonsingular, hence $M = AA^T$ and B are also nonsingular. So we can write

$$BB^T = AA^T \Rightarrow B^{-1}AA^T(B^{-1})^T = I$$

which implies that $B^{-1}A = R$ is orthogonal, since whenever a square matrix times its own transpose is the identity, the matrix is by definition orthogonal. This completes the proof. ∎

Now that we have learned A up to an unknown rotation, we can set out to use higher moments to learn the unknown rotation. First we will apply an affine transformation to our samples:

$$z = B^{-1}(y - b) = B^{-1}Ax = Rx$$

This is called *whitening* (think white noise), because it makes the first moments of our distribution zero and the second moments all one (in every direction). The key to our analysis is the following functional:

$$F(u) = \mathbb{E}[(u^T z)^4] = \mathbb{E}[(u^T Rx)^4]$$

We will want to minimize it over the unit sphere. As u ranges over the unit sphere, so does $v^T = u^T R$. Hence our optimization problem is equivalent to minimizing

$$H(v) = \mathbb{E}[(v^T x)^4]$$

over the unit sphere. This is a nonconvex optimization problem. In general, it is *NP*-hard to find the minimum or maximum of a nonconvex function. But it turns out that it is possible to find all *local minima* and that these are good enough to learn R.

Lemma 4.4.4 *If for all i, $\mathbb{E}[x_i^4] < 3$, then the only local minima of $H(v)$ are at $v = \pm e_i$, where e_i are the standard basis vectors.*

Proof: We can compute

$$
\begin{aligned}
\mathbb{E}\left[(v^T x)^4\right] &= \mathbb{E}\left[\sum_i (v_i x_i)^4 + 6 \sum_{i<j} (v_i x_i)^2 (v_j x_j)^2\right] \\
&= \sum_i v_i^4 \, \mathbb{E}(x_i^4) + 6 \sum_{i<j} v_i^2 v_j^2 + 3 \sum_i v_i^4 - 3 \sum_i v_i^4 \\
&= \sum_i v_i^4 \left(\mathbb{E}\left[x_i^4\right] - 3\right) + 3.
\end{aligned}
$$

From this expression, it is easy to check that the local minima of $H(v)$ correspond exactly to setting $v = \pm e_i$ for some i. ∎

Recall that $v^T = u^T R$, and so this characterization implies that the local minima of $F(u)$ correspond to setting u to be a column of $\pm R$. The algorithm proceeds by using gradient descent (and a lower bound on the Hessian) to show that you can find local minima of $F(u)$ quickly. The intuition is that if you keep following steep gradients, you decrease the objective value. Eventually, you must get stuck at a point where the gradients are small, which is an approximate local minimum. Any such u must be close to some column of $\pm R$, and we can then recurse on the orthogonal complement to the vector we have found to find the other columns of R. This idea requires some care to show that the errors do not accumulate too badly; see [74], [140], [17]. Note that when $\mathbb{E}[x_i^4] \neq 3$ instead of the stronger assumption that $\mathbb{E}[x_i^4] < 3$, we can follow the same approach, but we need to consider local minima and local maxima of $F(u)$. Also, Vempala and Xiao [140] gave an algorithm that works under weaker conditions whenever there is a constant order moment that is different from that of the standard Gaussian.

The strange expressions we encountered above are actually called *cumulants* and are an alternative basis for the moments of a distribution. Sometimes cumulants are easier to work with, since they satisfy the appealing property that the k-order cumulant of the sum of independent variables X_i and X_j is the sum of the k-order cumulants of X_i and X_j. This fact actually gives another more intuitive way to solve independent component analysis when combined with Jennrich's algorithm, but it involves a bit of a digression into higher-dimensional cumulants. We leave this as an exercise for the reader.

4.5 Exercises

Problem 4-1: Let $u \odot v$ denote the Khatri-Rao product between two vectors, where if $u \in \mathbb{R}^m$ and $v \in \mathbb{R}^n$, then $u \odot v \in \mathbb{R}^{mn}$ and corresponds to flattening the matrix uv^T into a vector, column by column. Also recall that the Kruskal rank k-rank of a collection of vectors $u_1, u_2, \ldots, u_m \in \mathbb{R}^n$ is the largest k such that *every* set of k vectors is linearly independent.

In this problem, we will explore properties of the Khatri-Rao product and use it to design algorithms for decomposing higher-order tensors.

(a) Let k_u and k_v be the k-rank of $u_1, u_2, \ldots, u_m$ and $v_1, v_2, \ldots, v_m$, respectively. Prove that the k-rank of $u_1 \odot v_1, u_2 \odot v_2, \ldots, u_m \odot v_m$ is at least $\min(k_u + k_v - 1, m)$.

(b) Construct a family of examples where the k-rank of $u_1 \odot u_1, u_2 \odot u_2, \ldots, u_m \odot u_m$ is exactly $2k_u - 1$, and not any larger. To make this nontrivial, you must use an example where $m > 2k_u - 1$.

(c) Given an $n \times n \times n \times n \times n$ fifth-order tensor $T = \sum_{i=1}^{r} a_i^{\otimes 5}$, give an algorithm for finding its factors that works for $r = 2n - 1$ under appropriate conditions on the factors $a_1, a_2, \ldots, a_r$. *Hint:* Reduce to the third-order case.

In fact, for random or perturbed vectors, the Khatri-Rao product has a much stronger effect of *multiplying* their Kruskal rank. These types of properties can be used to obtain algorithms for decomposing higher-order tensors in the highly overcomplete case where r is some polynomial in n.

Problem 4-2: In Section 4.4 we saw how to solve independent component analysis using nonconvex optimization. In this problem we will see how to solve it using tensor decomposition instead. Suppose we observe many samples of the form $y = Ax$, where A is an unknown nonsingular square matrix and each coordinate of x is independent and satisfies $\mathbb{E}[x_j] = 0$ and

$\mathbb{E}[x_j^4] \neq 3\,\mathbb{E}[x_j^2]^2$. The distribution of x_j is unknown and might not be the same for all j.

(a) Write down expressions for $\mathbb{E}[y^{\otimes 4}]$ and $\left(\mathbb{E}[y^{\otimes 2}]\right)^{\otimes 2}$ in terms of A and the moments of x. (You should not have any A's inside the expectation.)

(b) Using part (a), show how to use the moments of y to produce a tensor of the form $\sum_j c_j a_j^{\otimes 4}$, where a_j denotes column j of A and the c_j are nonzero scalars.

(c) Show how to recover the columns of A (up to permutation and scalar multiple) using Jennrich's algorithm.

5

Sparse Recovery

In this chapter, we will witness the power of *sparsity* for the first time. Let's get a sense of what it's good for. Consider the problem of solving an underdetermined linear system $Ax = b$. If we are given A and b, there's no chance to recover x uniquely, right? Well, not if we know that x is sparse. In that case, there are natural conditions on A where we actually will be able to recover x even though the number of rows of A is comparable to the sparsity of x rather than its dimension. Here we will cover the theory of sparse recovery. And in case you're curious, it's an area that not only has some theoretical gems, but also has had major practical impact.

5.1 Introduction

In signal processing (particularly imaging), we are often faced with the task of recovering some unknown signal given linear measurements of it. Let's fix our notation. Throughout this chapter, we will be interested in solving a linear system $Ax = b$ where A is an $m \times n$ matrix and x and b are n and m dimensional vectors, respectively. In our setup, both A and b are known. You can think of A as representing the input-output functionality of some measurement device we are using.

Now, if $m < n$, then we cannot hope to recover x uniquely. At best we could find some solution y that satisfies $Ay = b$ and we would have the promise that $x = y + z$, where z belongs to the kernel of A. This tells us that if we want to recover an n-dimensional signal, we need at least n linear measurements. This is quite natural. Sometimes you will hear this referred to as the Shannon-Nyquist rate, although I find that a rather opaque way to describe what is going on. The amazing idea that will save us is that if x is sparse — i.e., b is a linear combination of only a few columns of A — then we really will be able to get away with many fewer linear measurements and still be able to reconstruct x exactly.

What I want to do in this section is explain why you actually should not be surprised by it. If you ignore algorithms (which we won't do later on), it's actually quite simple. It turns out that assuming that x is sparse isn't enough by itself. We will always have to make some structural assumption about A as well. Let's consider the following notion:

Definition 5.1.1 *The Kruskal rank of a set of vectors $\{A_i\}_i$ is the maximum r such that all subsets of at most r vectors are linearly independent.*

If you are given a collection of n vectors in n dimensions, they can all be linearly independent, in which case their Kruskal rank is n. But if you have n vectors in m dimensions — like when we take the columns of our sensing matrix A – and m is smaller than n, the vectors can't be all linearly independent, but they can still have Kruskal rank m. In fact, this is the common case:

Claim 5.1.2 *If $A_1, A_2, \ldots, A_n$ are chosen uniformly at random from $\mathbb{S}^{m-1}$, then almost surely their Kruskal rank is m.*

Now let's prove our first main result about sparse recovery. Let $\|x\|_0$ be the number of nonzero entries of x. We will be interested in the following highly non-convex optimization problem:

$$(P_0) \qquad \min \|w\|_0 \text{ s.t. } Aw = b$$

Let's show that if we could solve (P_0), we could find x from much fewer than n linear measurements:

Lemma 5.1.3 *Let A be an $m \times n$ matrix whose columns have Kruskal rank at least r. Let x be an $r/2$-sparse vector and let $Ax = b$. Then the unique optimal solution to (P_0) is x.*

Proof: We know that x is a solution to $Ax = b$ that has objective value $\|x\|_0 = r/2$. Now suppose there were any other solution y that satisfies $Ay = b$.

Consider the difference between these solutions, i.e., $z = x - y$. We know that z is in the kernel of A. However, $\|z\|_0 \geq r + 1$, because by assumption every set of at most r columns of A is linearly independent. Finally, we have

$$\|y\|_0 \geq \|z\|_0 - \|x\|_0 \geq r/2 + 1$$

which implies that y has larger objective value than x. This completes the proof. ∎

So if we choose the columns of our sensing matrix to be random m dimensional vectors, then from just m linear measurements we can, in principle, recover any $m/2$-sparse vector uniquely. But there is a huge catch. Solving (P_0) — i.e., finding the sparsest solution to a system of linear equations — is NP-hard. In fact, this is a simple and important reduction that is worth seeing. Following Khachiyan [97], let's start from the subset sum problem, which is a standard NP-hard problem:

Problem 1 *Given distinct values $\alpha_1, \ldots, \alpha_n \in \mathbb{R}$, does there exist a set $I \subseteq [n]$ so that $|I| = m$ and $\sum_{i \in I} \alpha_i = 0$?*

We will embed an instance of this problem into the problem of finding the sparsest nonzero vector in a given subspace. We will make use of the following mapping, which is called the *weird moment curve*:

$$\Gamma'(\alpha_i) = [1, \alpha_i, \alpha_i^2, \ldots, \alpha_i^{m-2}, \alpha_i^m]$$

The difference between this and the standard moment curve is in the last term, where we have α_i^m instead of α_i^{m-1}.

Lemma 5.1.4 *A set I with $|I| = m$ has $\sum_{i \in I} \alpha_i = 0$ if and only if the vectors $\{\Gamma'(\alpha_i)\}_{i \in I}$ are linearly dependent.*

Proof: Consider the determinant of the matrix whose columns are $\{\Gamma'(\alpha_i)\}_{i \in I}$. Then the proof is based on the following observations:

(a) The determinant is a polynomial in the variables α_i with total degree $\binom{m}{2} + 1$, which can be seen by writing the determinant in terms of its Laplace expansion (see, e.g., [88]).

(b) Moreover, the determinant is divisible by $\prod_{i<j} \alpha_i - \alpha_j$, since the determinant is zero if any $\alpha_i = \alpha_j$.

Hence we can write the determinant as

$$\Big(\prod_{\substack{i<j \\ i,j \in I}} (\alpha_i - \alpha_j) \Big) \Big(\sum_{i \in I} \alpha_i \Big).$$

We have assumed that the α_i's are distinct, and consequently the determinant is zero if and only if the sum of $\alpha_i = 0$. ∎

We can now prove a double whammy. Not only is solving (P_0) NP-hard, but so is computing the Kruskal rank:

Theorem 5.1.5 *Both computing the Kruskal rank and finding the sparsest solution to a system of linear equations are NP-hard.*

Proof: First let's prove that computing the Kruskal rank is *NP*-hard. Consider the vectors $\{\Gamma'(\alpha_i)\}_i$. It follows from Lemma 5.1.4 that if there is a set I with $|I| = m$ that satisfies $\sum_{i \in I} \alpha_i = 0$, then the Kruskal rank of $\{\Gamma'(\alpha_i)\}_i$ is at most $m - 1$, and otherwise is exactly m. Since subset sum is *NP*-hard, so too is deciding whether the Kruskal rank is m or at most $m - 1$.

Now let's move on to showing that finding the sparsest solution to a linear system is *NP*-hard. We will use a one-to-many reduction. For each j, consider the following optimization problem:

$$(P_j) \quad \min \|w\|_0 \text{ s.t. } \Big[\Gamma'(\alpha_1), \ldots, \Gamma'(\alpha_{j-1}), \Gamma'(\alpha_{j+1}), \ldots, \Gamma'(\alpha_n)\Big] w = \Gamma'(\alpha_j)$$

It is easy to see that the Kruskal rank of $\{\Gamma'(\alpha_i)\}_i$ is at most $m - 1$ if and only if there is some j so that (P_j) has a solution whose objective value is at most $m - 2$. Thus (P_0) is also *NP*-hard. ∎

In the rest of this chapter, we will focus on algorithms. We will give simple greedy methods as well as ones based on convex programming relaxations. These algorithms will work under more stringent assumptions on the sensing matrix A than just that its columns have large Kruskal rank. Nevertheless, all of the assumptions we make will still be met by a randomly chosen A, as well as many others. The algorithms we give will even come with stronger guarantees that are meaningful in the presence of noise.

5.2 Incoherence and Uncertainty Principles

In 1965, Logan [107] discovered a striking phenomenon. If you take a band-limited signal and corrupt it at a sparse set of locations, it is possible to uniquely recover the original signal. This turns out to be a sparse recovery problem in disguise. Let's formalize this:

Example 1 *The spikes-and-sines matrix A is an $n \times 2n$ matrix*

$$A = [I, D]$$

where I is the identity matrix and D is the discrete Fourier transform matrix, i.e.,

$$D_{a,b} = \frac{\omega^{(a-1)(b-1)}}{\sqrt{n}}$$

and $\omega = e^{2\pi i/n}$ is the nth root of unity.

Let x be a sparse $2n$-dimensional vector. The nonzeros in the first n coordinates represent the locations of the corruptions. The nonzeros in the last

n coordinates represent the frequencies present in the original signal. Thus we know A and b and are promised that there is a solution x to $Ax = b$ where x is sparse. It took a number of years until the work of Donoho and Stark [64], who realized that this phenomenon wasn't limited to just the spike-and-sines matrix. It's actually a quite general phenomenon. The key is the notion of incoherence:

Definition 5.2.1 *The columns of* $A \in \mathbb{R}^{n \times m}$ *are* μ*-incoherent if for all* $i \neq j$

$$|\langle A_i, A_j \rangle| \leq \mu \|A_i\| \cdot \|A_j\|.$$

Throughout this section, we will focus on just the case when the columns of A are unit vectors. Hence a matrix is μ-incoherent if for all $i \neq j$, $|\langle A_i, A_j \rangle| \leq \mu$. However, all the results we derive here can be extended to general A when the columns are not necessarily unit vectors. As we did for the Kruskal rank, let's show that random vectors are incoherent:

Claim 5.2.2 *If* $A_1, A_2, \ldots, A_m$ *are chosen uniformly at random from* $\mathbb{S}^{n-1}$, *then with high probability they will be* μ*-incoherent for*

$$\mu = O\left(\sqrt{\frac{\log m}{n}}\right).$$

You can also check that the spike-and-sines matrix is μ-incoherent with $\mu = 1/\sqrt{n}$. In that way, the results we derive here will contain Logan's phenomenon as a special case. Anyway, let's now show that if A is incoherent and if x is sparse enough, then it will be the uniquely sparsest solution to $Ax = b$.

Lemma 5.2.3 *Let* A *be an* $n \times m$ *matrix that is* μ*-incoherent and whose columns are unit norm. If* $Ax = b$ *and* $\|x\|_0 < \frac{1}{2\mu}$, *then* x *is the uniquely sparsest solution to the linear system.*

Proof: Suppose for the sake of contradiction that we have another solution y that satisfies $Ay = b$ and $\|y\|_0 < \frac{1}{2\mu}$. Then we can look at the difference between these solutions, i.e., $z = x - y$, which satisfies $\|z\|_0 < \frac{1}{\mu}$ and consider the expression

$$z^T A^T A z = 0.$$

If we let S denote the support of z — i.e., the locations where it is nonzero — we have that $A^T A$ restricted to the rows and columns in S is singular. Let this matrix be B. Then B has ones along the diagonal, and the entries off the diagonal are bounded by μ in absolute value. But by Gershgorin's disk theorem, we know that all the eigenvalues of B are contained in a disk in the complex plane centered at one with radius $\mu|S| < 1$. Thus B is nonsingular and we have a contradiction. ∎

Actually, we can prove a stronger uniqueness result when A is the union of two orthonormal bases, as is the case for the spikes-and-sines matrix. Let's first prove the following result, which we will mysteriously call an uncertainty principle:

Lemma 5.2.4 *Let $A = [U, V]$ be an $n \times 2n$ matrix that is μ-incoherent where U and V are $n \times n$ orthogonal matrices. If $b = U\alpha = V\beta$, then $\|\alpha\|_0 + \|\beta\|_0 \geq \frac{2}{\mu}$.*

Proof: Since U and V are orthonormal, we have that $\|b\|_2 = \|\alpha\|_2 = \|\beta\|_2$. We can rewrite b as either $U\alpha$ or $V\beta$, and hence $\|b\|_2^2 = |\beta^T(V^TU)\alpha|$. Because A is incoherent, we can conclude that each entry of V^TU has absolute value at most $\mu(A)$, and so $|\beta^T(V^TU)\alpha| \leq \mu(A)\|\alpha\|_1\|\beta\|_1$. Using Cauchy-Schwarz, it follows that $\|\alpha\|_1 \leq \sqrt{\|\alpha\|_0}\|\alpha\|_2$ and thus

$$\|b\|_2^2 \leq \mu(A)\sqrt{\|\alpha\|_0\|\beta\|_0}\|\alpha\|_2\|\beta\|_2.$$

Rearranging, we have $\frac{1}{\mu(A)} \leq \sqrt{\|\alpha\|_0\|\beta\|_0}$. Finally, applying the AM-GM inequality, we get $\frac{2}{\mu} \leq \|\alpha\|_0 + \|\beta\|_0$ and this completes the proof. ∎

This proof was short and simple. Perhaps the only confusing part is why we called it an uncertainty principle. Let's give an application of Lemma 5.2.4 to clarify this point. If we set A to be the spikes-and-sines matrix, we get that any non-zero signal must have at least $\sqrt{n}$ nonzeros in the standard basis or in the Fourier basis. What this means is that no signal can be sparse in both the time and frequency domains simultaneously! It's worth taking a step back. If we had just proven this result, you would have naturally associated it with the Heisenberg uncertainty principle. But it turns out that what's really driving it is just the incoherence of the time and frequency bases for our signal, and it applies equally well to many other pairs of bases.

Let's use our uncertainty principle to prove an even stronger uniqueness result:

Claim 5.2.5 *Let $A = [U, V]$ be an $n \times 2n$ matrix that is μ-incoherent where U and V are $n \times n$ orthogonal matrices. If $Ax = b$ and $\|x\|_0 < \frac{1}{\mu}$, then x is the uniquely sparsest solution to the linear system.*

Proof: Consider any alternative solution $A\widetilde{x} = b$. Set $y = x - \widetilde{x}$, in which case $y \in \ker(A)$. Write y as $y = [\alpha_y, \beta_y]^T$, and since $Ay = 0$, we have that $U\alpha_y = -V\beta_y$. We can now apply the uncertainty principle and conclude that $\|y\|_0 = \|\alpha_y\|_0 + \|\beta_y\|_0 \geq \frac{2}{\mu}$. It is easy to see that $\|\widetilde{x}\|_0 \geq \|y\|_0 - \|x\|_0 > \frac{1}{\mu}$, and so $\widetilde{x}$ has strictly more nonzeros than x does, and this completes the proof. ∎

We can connect incoherence back to our original discussion about Kruskal rank. It turns out that having a matrix whose columns are incoherent is just one easy-to-check way to certify a lower bound on the Kruskal rank. The proof of the following claim is essentially the same as the proof of Lemma 5.2.3. We leave it as an exercise for the reader.

Claim 5.2.6 *If A is μ-incoherent, then the Kruskal rank of the columns of A is at least $1/\mu$.*

In the next section, we will give a simple greedy algorithm for solving sparse recovery problems on incoherent matrices. The way the algorithm will certify that it is making progress and finding the right nonzero locations of x as it goes along will revolve around the same ideas that underlie the uniqueness results we just proved.

5.3 Pursuit Algorithms

There is an important class of algorithms for sparse recovery problems called pursuit algorithms. These algorithms are greedy and iterative. They work with incoherent matrices and look for the column in A that explains as much of the observed vector b as possible. They subtract off a multiple of that column and continue on the remainder. The first such algorithm was introduced in an influential paper of Mallat and Zhang [111] and was called matching pursuit. In this section, we will analyze a variant of it called *orthogonal matching pursuit*. What's particularly convenient about the latter is that the algorithm will maintain the invariant that the remainder is orthogonal to all the columns of A we have selected so far. This is more expensive in each step, but is easier to analyze and understand the intuition behind.

Throughout this section, let A be an $n \times m$ matrix that is μ-incoherent. Let x be k-sparse with $k < 1/(2\mu)$ and let $Ax = b$. Finally, we will use T to denote the support of x — i.e., the locations of the nonzeros in x. Now let's formally define orthogonal matching pursuit:

Orthogonal Matching Pursuit

Input: matrix $A \in \mathbb{R}^{n \times m}$, vector $b \in \mathbb{R}^n$, desired number of nonzero entries $k \in \mathbb{N}$

Output: solution x with at most k nonzero entries

Initialize: $x^0 = 0$, $r^0 = Ax^0 - b$, $S = \emptyset$
For $\ell = 1, 2, \ldots, k$
    Choose column j that maximizes $\frac{|\langle A_j, r^{\ell-1} \rangle|}{\|A_j\|_2^2}$.
Add j to S.
    Set $r^\ell = \text{proj}_{U^\perp}(b)$, where $U = \text{span}(A_S)$.
    If $r^\ell = 0$, break.
End
Solve for x_S: $A_S x_S = b$. Set $x_{\bar{S}} = 0$.

Our anlaysis will focus on establishing the following two invariants:

(a) Each index j the algorithm selects is in T.
(b) Each index j gets chosen at most once.

These two properties immediately imply that orthogonal matching pursuit recovers the true solution x, because the residual error r^ℓ will be nonzero until $S = T$, and moreover, the linear system $A_T x_T = b$ has a unique solution (which we know from the previous section).

Property **(b)** is straightforward, because once $j \in S$ at every subsequent step in the algorithm, we will have that $r^\ell \perp U$, where $U = \text{span}(A_S)$, so $\langle r^\ell, A_j \rangle = 0$ if $j \in S$. Our main goal is to establish property **(a)**, which we will prove inductively. The main lemma is:

Lemma 5.3.1 *If $S \subseteq T$ at the start of a stage, then orthogonal matching pursuit selects $j \in T$.*

We will first prove a helper lemma:

Lemma 5.3.2 *If $r^{\ell-1}$ is supported in T at the start of a stage, then orthogonal matching pursuit selects $j \in T$.*

Proof: Let $r^{\ell-1} = \sum_{i \in T} y_i A_i$. Then we can reorder the columns of A so that the first k' columns correspond to the k' nonzero entries of y, in decreasing order of magnitude:

$$\underbrace{|y_1| \geq |y_2| \geq \cdots \geq |y_{k'}| > 0,}_{\text{corresponds to first } k' \text{ columns of } A} \quad |y_{k'+1}| = 0, |y_{k'+2}| = 0, \ldots, |y_m| = 0$$

where $k' \leq k$. Hence $\text{supp}(y) = \{1, 2, \ldots, k'\} \subseteq T$. Then, to ensure that we pick $j \in T$, a sufficient condition is that

$$|\langle A_1, r^{\ell-1} \rangle| > |\langle A_i, r^{\ell-1} \rangle| \qquad \text{for all } i \geq k' + 1. \tag{5.1}$$

We can lower-bound the left-hand side of (5.1):

$$|\langle r^{\ell-1}, A_1\rangle| = \left|\left\langle \sum_{\ell=1}^{k'} y_\ell A_\ell, A_1\right\rangle\right| \geq |y_1| - \sum_{\ell=2}^{k'} |y_\ell||\langle A_\ell, A_1\rangle|$$

$$\geq |y_1| - |y_1|(k'-1)\mu \geq |y_1|(1 - k'\mu + \mu),$$

which, under the assumption that $k' \leq k < 1/(2\mu)$, is strictly lower-bounded by $|y_1|(1/2 + \mu)$.

We can then upper-bound the right-hand side of (5.1):

$$|\langle r^{\ell-1}, A_i\rangle| = \left|\left\langle \sum_{\ell=1}^{k'} y_\ell A_\ell, A_i\right\rangle\right| \leq |y_1| \sum_{\ell=1}^{k'} |\langle A_\ell, A_i\rangle| \leq |y_1|k'\mu,$$

which, under the assumption that $k' \leq k < 1/(2\mu)$, is strictly upper-bounded by $|y_1|/2$. Since $|y_1|(1/2+\mu) > |y_1|/2$, we conclude that condition (5.1) holds, guaranteeing that the algorithm selects $j \in T$, and this completes the proof. ∎

Now we can prove Lemma 5.3.1:

Proof: Suppose that $S \subseteq T$ at the start of a stage. Then the residual $r^{\ell-1}$ is supported in T, because we can write it as

$$r^{\ell-1} = b - \sum_{i \in S} z_i A_i, \text{ where } z = \arg\min \|b - A_S z_S\|_2.$$

Applying the above lemma, we conclude that the algorithm selects $j \in T$. ∎

This establishes property **(a)** inductively and completes the proof of correctness for orthogonal matching pursuit, which we summarize below:

Theorem 5.3.3 *Let A be an $n \times m$ matrix that is μ-incoherent and whose columns are unit norm. If $Ax = b$ and $\|x\|_0 < \frac{1}{2\mu}$, then the output of orthogonal matching pursuit is exactly x.*

Note that this algorithm works up to exactly the threshold where we established uniqueness. However, in the case where $A = [U, V]$ and U and V are orthogonal, we proved a uniqueness result that is better by a constant factor. There is no known algorithm that matches the best known uniqueness bound there, although there are better algorithms than the one above (see, e.g., [67]).

It is also worth mentioning how other pursuit algorithms differ. For example, in matching pursuit we do not recompute the coefficients x_i for $i \in S$ at the end of each stage. We just keep whatever they are set to and hope that they do not need to be adjusted much when we add a new index j to S.

This is what makes matching pursuit faster in practice; however, the analysis is more cumbersome because we need to keep track of how the error (due to not projecting b on the orthogonal complement of the columns we've chosen so far) accumulates.

5.4 Prony's Method

There is a widespread misconception that sparse recovery algorithms are a modern invention. Actually, sparse recovery dates back to 1795, to an algorithm called Prony's method. It will give us almost everything we want. We will have an explicit $2k \times n$ sensing matrix A for which we will be able to recover any k-sparse signal exactly and with an efficient algorithm. It even has the benefit that we can compute the matrix-vector product Ax in $O(n \log n)$ time using the fast Fourier transform.

The caveat to this method is that it is very unstable, since it involves inverting a Vandermonde matrix, which can be very ill-conditioned. So when you hear about compressed sensing as breaking the Shannon-Nyquist barrier, you should remember that Prony's method already does that. What sets apart the algorithms we will study later on is that they work in the presence of noise. That's the crucial aspect that makes them so practically relevant. Nevertheless, Prony's method is very useful from a theoretical standpoint, and the types of results you can get out of it have a habit of being rediscovered under other names.

Properties of the Discrete Fourier Transform

Prony's method will make crucial use of various properties of the discrete Fourier transform. Recall that as a matrix, this transformation has entries

$$F_{a,b} = \left(\frac{1}{\sqrt{n}} \right) \exp \left(\frac{i2\pi (a - 1)(b - 1)}{n} \right).$$

As we did before, we will simplify the notation and write $\omega = e^{i2\pi/n}$ for the nth root of unity. With this notation, the entry in row a, column b is $\omega^{(a-1)(b-1)}$.

The matrix F has a number of important properties, including:

(a) F is orthonormal: $F^H F = FF^H$, where F^H is the Hermitian transpose of F.

(b) F diagonalizes the convolution operator.

We haven't defined convolution, so let's do that now. Actually, let's do that through its corresponding linear transformation:

Definition 5.4.1 (Circulant matrix) *For a vector* $c = [c_1, c_2, \ldots, c_n]$, *let*

$$M^c = \begin{bmatrix} c_n & c_{n-1} & c_{n-2} & \cdots & c_1 \\ c_1 & c_n & c_{n-1} & \cdots & c_2 \\ \vdots & & & & \vdots \\ c_{n-1} & \cdots & \cdots & \cdots & c_n \end{bmatrix}.$$

Then the matrix-vector product $M^c x$ is the vector we get out of convolving c and x, which we will denote by $c * x$. Intuitively, if you think of c and x as representing the probability distribution of discrete random variables, then $c * x$ represents the distribution of the random variable you get by adding the two of them and wrapping around n using modular arithmetic.

As we asserted above, we can diagonalize M^c using F. More formally, we have the following fact, which we will use without proof:

Claim 5.4.2 $M^c = F^H diag(\widehat{c})F$, *where* $\widehat{c} = Fc$.

This tells us that we can think of convolution as coordinate-wise multiplication in the Fourier representation. More precisely:

Corollary 5.4.3 *Let* $z = c * x$; *then* $\widehat{z} = \widehat{c} \odot \widehat{x}$, *where* $\odot$ *indicates coordinate-wise multiplication.*

Proof: We can write $z = M^c x = F^H diag(\widehat{c})Fx = F^H diag(\widehat{c})\widehat{x} = F^H(\widehat{c} \odot \widehat{x})$, and this completes the proof. ∎

The helper Polynomial

Prony's method revolves around the following helper polynomial:

Definition 5.4.4 (helper polynomial)

$$p(z) = \prod_{b \in supp(x)} \omega^{-b}(\omega^b - z)$$

$$= 1 + \lambda_1 z + \ldots + \lambda_k z^k$$

Claim 5.4.5 *If we know $p(z)$, we can find $supp(x)$.*

Proof: In fact, an index b is in the support of x if and only if $p(\omega^b) = 0$. So we can evaluate p at powers of ω, and the exponents where p evaluates to a nonzero are exactly the support of x. ∎

The basic idea of Prony's method is to use the first $2k$ values of the discrete Fourier transform to find p, and hence the support of x. We can then solve a linear system to actually find the values of x. Our first goal is to find the helper polynomial. Let

$$v = [1, \lambda_1, \lambda_2, \ldots, \lambda_k, 0, \ldots, 0], \text{ and } \widehat{v} = Fv.$$

It is easy to see that the value of $\widehat{v}$ at index $b + 1$ is exactly $p(\omega^b)$.

Claim 5.4.6 $supp(\widehat{v}) = \overline{supp(x)}$

That is, the zeros of $\widehat{v}$ correspond to the roots of p, and hence nonzeros of x. Conversely, the nonzeros of $\widehat{v}$ correspond to the zeros of x. We conclude that $x \odot \widehat{v} = 0$, and so:

Corollary 5.4.7 $M^{\widehat{x}} v = 0$

Proof: We can apply Claim 5.4.2 to rewrite $x \odot \widehat{v} = 0$ as $\widehat{x} * v = \widehat{0} = 0$, and this implies the corollary. ∎

Let us write out this linear system explicitly:

$$M^{\widehat{x}} = \begin{bmatrix} \widehat{x}_n & \widehat{x}_{n-1} & \ldots & \widehat{x}_{n-k} & \ldots & \widehat{x}_1 \\ \widehat{x}_1 & \widehat{x}_n & \ldots & \widehat{x}_{n-k+1} & \ldots & \widehat{x}_2 \\ \vdots & \vdots & \vdots & \vdots & \vdots & \vdots \\ \widehat{x}_{k+1} & \widehat{x}_k & \ldots & \widehat{x}_1 & \ldots & \widehat{x}_{k+2} \\ \vdots & \vdots & \vdots & \vdots & \vdots & \vdots \\ \widehat{x}_{2k} & \widehat{x}_{2k-1} & \ldots & \widehat{x}_k & \ldots & \widehat{x}_{2k+1} \\ \vdots & \vdots & \vdots & \vdots & \vdots & \vdots \end{bmatrix}$$

Recall, we do not have access to all the entries of this matrix, since we are only given the first $2k$ values of the DFT of x. However, consider the $k \times k + 1$ submatrix whose top left value is $\widehat{x}_{k+1}$ and whose bottom right value is $\widehat{x}_k$. This matrix only involves the values that we do know!

Consider

$$\begin{bmatrix} \widehat{x}_k & \widehat{x}_{k-1} & \ldots & \widehat{x}_1 \\ \vdots & & & \\ \widehat{x}_{2k-1} & \widehat{x}_{2k-1} & \ldots & \widehat{x}_k \end{bmatrix} \begin{bmatrix} \lambda_1 \\ \lambda_2 \\ \vdots \\ \lambda_k \end{bmatrix} = - \begin{bmatrix} \widehat{x}_{k+1} \\ \vdots \\ \vdots \\ \widehat{x}_{2k} \end{bmatrix}$$

It turns out that this linear system is full rank, so λ is the unique solution to the linear system (the proof is left to the reader[1]). The entries in λ are the coefficients of p, so once we solve for λ, we can evaluate the helper polynomial on ω^b to find the support of x. All that remains is to find the values of x. Indeed, let M be the restriction of F to the columns in S and its first $2k$ rows. M is a Vandermonde matrix, so again $Mx_S = \hat{x}_{1,2,\ldots,2k}$ has a unique solution, and we can solve this linear system to find the nonzero values of x.

The guarantees of Prony's method are summarized in the following theorem:

Theorem 5.4.8 *Let A be the $2k \times n$ matrix obtained from taking the first $2k$ rows of the discrete Fourier transform matrix F. Then for any k-sparse signal x, Prony's method recovers x exactly from Ax.*

In case you're curious, this is yet another topic in sparse recovery that we can relate back to Kruskal rank. It is easy to show that the columns of A have Kruskal rank equal to $2k$. In fact, this is true regardless of which $2k$ rows of F we choose. Moreover, it turns out that there are settings where Prony's method and related methods can be shown to work in the presence of noise, but only under some separation conditions on the nonzero locations in x. See Moitra [113] for further details.

5.5 Compressed Sensing

In this section we will introduce a powerful new assumption about our sensing matrix A, called the restricted isometry property. You can think of it as a robust analogue of the Kruskal rank, where not only do we want every set of (say) $2k$ columns of A to be linearly independent, we also want them to be well-conditioned. We will show that a simple convex programming relaxation is amazingly effective. With a good choice for A, we will be able to recover a k-sparse signal from $O(k \log(n/k))$ linear measurements. The algorithm runs in polynomial time and, moreover, it is robust to noise in the sense that even if x is not k-sparse, we will still be able to approximately recover its k largest coordinates. This is a much stronger type of guarantee. After all, natural signals aren't k-sparse. But being able to recover their k largest coordinates is often good enough.

Now let's define the restricted isometry property:

Definition 5.5.1 *A matrix A satisfies the (k, δ)-restricted isometry property if for all k-sparse vectors x we have*

$$(1 - \delta)\|x\|_2^2 \leq \|Ax\|_2^2 \leq (1 + \delta)\|x\|_2^2.$$

As with the other assumptions we have considered, the restricted isometry property holds on randomly chosen sensing matrices with high probability:

Lemma 5.5.2 *Let A be an $m \times n$ matrix where each entry is an independent standard Gaussian random variable. Provided that $m \geq 10k \log n/k$, then with high probability A satisfies the $(k, 1/3)$-restricted isometry property.*

Next let's work toward formalizing what we mean by approximately recovering the k largest coordinates of x. Our goal will be formulated in terms of the following function:

Definition 5.5.3 $\gamma_k(x) = \min_w$ *s.t.* $\|w\|_0 \leq k$ $\|x - w\|_1$

To put this in more plain terms, $\gamma_k(x)$ is the sum of the absolute values of all but the k largest magnitude entries of x. And if x really is k-sparse, then $\gamma_k(x) = 0$.

Our goal is to find a w that approximates x almost as well as any k-sparse vector does. More formally, we want to find a w that satisfies $\|x - w\|_1 \leq C\gamma_k(x)$, and we want to do so using as few linear measurements as possible. This learning goal already subsumes our other exact recovery results from previous sections, because when x is k-sparse, then, as we discussed, $\gamma_k(x)$ is zero, so we have no choice but to recover $w = x$.

In this section, our approach will be based on a convex programming relaxation. Instead of trying to solve the NP-hard optimization problem (P_0), we will consider the now famous ℓ_1-relaxation:

$$(P_1) \qquad \min \|w\|_1 \text{ s.t. } Aw = b$$

Let's first state some of the well-known results about using (P_1) for sparse recovery:

Theorem 5.5.4 *[43] If $\delta_{2k} + \delta_{3k} < 1$, then if $\|x\|_0 \leq k$, we have $w = x$.*

Theorem 5.5.5 *[42] If $\delta_{3k} + 3\delta_{4k} < 2$, then*

$$\|x - w\|_2 \leq \frac{C}{\sqrt{k}} \gamma_k(x).$$

The guarantees above are a bit different (and often stronger) than the others, because the bound is in terms of the ℓ_2 norm of the error $x - w$.

Theorem 5.5.6 *[51] If $\delta_{2k} < 1/3$, then*

$$\|x - w\|_1 \leq \frac{2 + 2\delta_{2k}}{1 - 3\delta_{2k}} \gamma_k(x).$$

We won't prove exactly these results. But we will prove something similar following the approach of Kashin and Temlyakov [96], which (to my taste) greatly streamlines these analyses. But before we get to analyzing (P_1), we need to introduce a notion from functional analysis called an almost Euclidean subsection.

Almost Euclidean Subsections

Informally, an almost Euclidean subsection is a subspace where the ℓ_1 and ℓ_2 norms are almost equivalent after rescaling. We will just assert the fact that a random subspace is an almost Euclidean subsection with high probability. Instead, we will spend most of our time establishing various geometric properties about Euclidean subsections that we will use when we return to compressed sensing. The crucial definition is the following:

Definition 5.5.7 *A subspace $\Gamma \subseteq \mathbb{R}^n$ is a C-almost Euclidean subsection if for all $v \in \Gamma$,*

$$\frac{1}{\sqrt{n}}\|v\|_1 \leq \|v\|_2 \leq \frac{C}{\sqrt{n}}\|v\|_1.$$

Actually, the first inequality is trivial. For any vector, it's always true that $\frac{1}{\sqrt{n}}\|v\|_1 \leq \|v\|_2$. The action is all happening in the second inequality. The first time you see them, it's not obvious that such subspaces exist. Indeed, Garnaev and Gluskin [75] proved that there are plenty of almost Euclidean subsections:

Theorem 5.5.8 *If Γ is a subspace chosen uniformly at random with $dim(\Gamma) = n - m$, then for*

$$C = O\left(\sqrt{\frac{n}{m}} \log \frac{n}{m}\right)$$

we have that Γ will be a C-almost Euclidean subsection with high probability.

Let's end with a nice picture to keep in mind. Consider the unit ball for the ℓ_1 norm. It's sometimes called the cross polytope, and to visualize it you can think of it as the convex hull of the vectors $\{\pm e_i\}_i$ where e_i are the standard basis vectors. Then a subspace Γ is almost Euclidean if, when we intersect it and the cross polytope, we get a convex body that is almost spherical.

Geometric Properties of Γ

Here we will establish some important geometric properties of C-almost Euclidean subsections. Throughout this section, let $S = n/C^2$. First we show that Γ cannot contain any sparse, nonzero vectors:

Claim 5.5.9 *Let $v \in \Gamma$, then either $v = 0$ or $|supp(v)| \geq S$.*

Proof: From Cauchy-Schwartz and the C-almost Euclidean property, we have

$$\|v\|_1 = \sum_{j\in\text{supp}(v)} |v_j| \le \sqrt{|\text{supp}(v)|} \cdot \|v\|_2 \le \sqrt{|\text{supp}(v)|}\frac{C}{\sqrt{n}}\|v\|_1.$$

The proof now follows from rearranging terms. ∎

It's worth noting that there is a nice analogy with linear error correcting codes, which are also subspaces of large dimension (but over GF_2), where we want every nonzero vector to have at least a constant fraction of its coordinates be nonzero. In any case, let's move on to some even stronger properties of almost Euclidean subsections, which have to do with how well the ℓ_1 norm is spread out. First let's give a useful piece of notation:

Definition 5.5.10 *For $\Lambda \subseteq [n]$, let v_Λ denote the restriction of v to coordinates in Λ. Similarly, let v^Λ denote the restriction of v to $\overline{\Lambda}$.*

With this notation in hand, let's prove the following:

Claim 5.5.11 *Suppose $v \in \Gamma$ and $\Lambda \subseteq [n]$ and $|\Lambda| < S/16$. Then*

$$\|v_\Lambda\|_1 < \frac{\|v\|_1}{4}.$$

Proof: The proof is almost identical to that of Claim 5.5.9. Again using Cauchy-Schwartz and the C-almost Euclidean property, we have

$$\|v_\Lambda\|_1 \le \sqrt{|\Lambda|}\|v_\Lambda\|_2 \le \sqrt{|\Lambda|}\|v\|_2 \le \sqrt{|\Lambda|}\frac{C}{\sqrt{n}}\|v\|_1,$$

which, plugging in terms, completes the proof. ∎

And now we have all the tools we need to give our first results about (P_1):

Lemma 5.5.12 *Let $w = x + v$ and $v \in \Gamma$, where $\|x\|_0 \le S/16$. Then $\|w\|_1 > \|x\|_1$.*

Proof: Set $\Lambda = \text{supp}(x)$. Then

$$\|w\|_1 = \|(x+v)_\Lambda\|_1 + \|(x+v)^\Lambda\|_1 = \|(x+v)_\Lambda\|_1 + \|v^\Lambda\|_1.$$

Now we can invoke triangle inequality:

$$\|w\|_1 \ge \|x_\Lambda\|_1 - \|v_\Lambda\|_1 + \|v^\Lambda\|_1 = \|x\|_1 - \|v_\Lambda\|_1 + \|v^\Lambda\|_1 = x_\Lambda\|_1 - 2\|v_\Lambda\|_1 + \|v\|_1$$

However, $\|v\|_1 - 2\|v_\Lambda\|_1 \ge \|v\|_1/2 > 0$ using Claim 5.5.11. This completes the proof. ∎

Plugging in the bounds from Theorem 5.5.8, we have shown that we can recover a k-sparse vector x of dimension n with

$$k \leq S/16 = \Omega(n/C^2) = \Omega\left(\frac{m}{\log n/m}\right)$$

from m linear measurements.

Next we will consider stable recovery. Our main theorem is:

Theorem 5.5.13 *Let* $\Gamma = ker(A)$ *be a C-almost Euclidean subsection. Let* $S = \frac{n}{C^2}$. *If* $Ax = Aw = b$ *and* $\|w\|_1 \leq \|x\|_1$, *we have*

$$\|x - w\|_1 \leq 4 \sigma_{\frac{S}{16}}(x).$$

Proof: Let $\Lambda \subseteq [n]$ be the set of $S/16$ coordinates maximizing $\|x_\Lambda\|_1$. We want to upper-bound $\|x - w\|_1$. By repeated application of the triangle inequality, $\|w\|_1 = \|w^\Lambda\|_1 + \|w_\Lambda\|_1 \leq \|x\|_1$, and the definition of $\sigma_t(\cdot)$, it follows that

$$\begin{aligned}
\|x - w\|_1 &= \|(x - w)_\Lambda\|_1 + \|(x - w)^\Lambda\|_1 \\
&\leq \|(x - w)_\Lambda\|_1 + \|x^\Lambda\|_1 + \|w^\Lambda\|_1 \\
&\leq \|(x - w)_\Lambda\|_1 + \|x^\Lambda\|_1 + \|x\|_1 - \|w_\Lambda\|_1 \\
&\leq 2\|(x - w)_\Lambda\|_1 + 2\|x^\Lambda\|_1 \\
&\leq 2\|(x - w)_\Lambda\|_1 + 2\sigma_{\frac{S}{16}}(x).
\end{aligned}$$

Since $(x - w) \in \Gamma$, we can apply Claim 5.5.11 to conclude that $\|(x-w)_\Lambda\|_1 \leq \frac{1}{4}\|x - w\|_1$. Hence

$$\|x - w\|_1 \leq \frac{1}{2}\|x - w\|_1 + 2\sigma_{\frac{S}{16}}(x).$$

This completes the proof. ∎

Epilogue

Finally, we will end with one of the main open questions in compressed sensing, which is to give a *deterministic* construction of matrices that satisfy the restricted isometry property:

Question 7 (Open) *Is there a deterministic algorithm to construct a matrix with the restricted isometry property? Alternatively, is there a deterministic algorithm to construct an almost Euclidean subsection* Γ *?*

Avi Wigderson likes to refer to these types of problems as "finding hay in a haystack." We know that a randomly chosen A satisfies the restricted isometry property with high probability. Its kernel is also an almost Euclidean subspace with high probability. But can we remove the randomness? The best known deterministic construction is due to Guruswami, Lee, and Razborov [82]:

Theorem 5.5.14 *[82] There is a polynomial time deterministic algorithm for constructing an almost Euclidean subspace* Γ *with parameter* $C \sim (\log n)^{\log \log \log n}$.

This has got to be too strange a bound to be the best we can do, right?

5.6 Exercises

Problem 5-1: In this question, we will explore uniqueness conditions for sparse recovery and conditions under which ℓ_1-minimization provably works.

(a) Let $A\widehat{x} = b$, and suppose A has n columns. Further suppose $2k \le m$. Prove that for *every* $\widehat{x}$ with $\|\widehat{x}\|_0 \le k$, $\widehat{x}$ is the uniquely sparsest solution to the linear system if and only if the k-rank of the columns of A is at least $2k$.

(b) Let $U = \text{kernel}(A)$, and $U \subset \mathbb{R}^n$. Suppose that for each nonzero $x \in U$, and for any set $S \subset [n]$ with $|S| \le k$,

$$\|x_S\|_1 < \frac{1}{2}\|x\|_1$$

where x_S denotes the restriction of x to the coordinates in S. Prove that

$$(P1) \qquad \min \|x\|_1 \text{ s.t. } Ax = b$$

recovers $x = \widehat{x}$, provided that $A\widehat{x} = b$ and $\|\widehat{x}\|_0 \le k$.

(c) **Challenge:** Can you construct a subspace $U \subset \mathbb{R}^n$ of dimension $\Omega(n)$ that has the property that every nonzero $x \in U$ has at least $\Omega(n)$ nonzero coordinates? *Hint:* Use an expander.

Problem 5-2: Let $\widehat{x}$ be a k-sparse vector in n-dimensions. Let ω be the nth root of unity. Suppose we are given $v_\ell = \sum_{j=1}^n \widehat{x}_j \omega^{\ell j}$ for $\ell = 0, 1, \ldots, 2k - 1$. Let $A, B \in \mathbb{R}^{k \times k}$ be defined so that $A_{i,j} = v_{i+j-2}$ and $B_{i,j} = v_{i+j-1}$.

(a) Express both A and B in the form $A = VD_A V^T$ and $B = VD_B V^T$, where V is a Vandermonde matrix and D_A, D_B are diagonal.

(b) Prove that the solutions to the generalized eigenvalue problem $Ax = \lambda Bx$ can be used to recover the locations of the nonzeros in $\widehat{x}$.

(c) Given the locations of the nonzeros in $\widehat{x}$ and $v_0, v_1, \ldots, v_{k-1}$, give an algorithm to recover the values of the nonzero coefficients in $\widehat{x}$.

This is called the matrix pencil method. If you squint, it looks like Prony's method (Section 5.4) and has similar guarantees. Both are (somewhat) robust to noise if and only if the Vandermonde matrix is well-conditioned, and exactly when that happens is a longer story. See Moitra [113].

6

Sparse Coding

Many types of signals turn out to be sparse, either in their natural basis or in a hand-designed basis (e.g., a family of wavelets). But if we are given a collection of signals and we don't know the basis in which they are sparse, can we automatically learn it? This problem goes by various names, including sparse coding and dictionary learning. It was introduced in the context of neuroscience, where it was used to explain how neurons get the types of activation patterns they have. It also has applications to compression and deep learning. In this chapter, we will give algorithms for sparse coding that leverage convex programming relaxations as well as iterative algorithms where we will prove that greedy methods successfully minimize a nonconvex function in an appropriate stochastic model.

6.1 Introduction

Sparse coding was introduced by Olshausen and Field [117], who were neuroscientists interested in understanding properties of the mammalian visual cortex. They were able to measure the receptive field of neurons — essentially how neurons respond to various types of stimuli. But what they found surprised them. The response patterns were always

(a) *spatially localized*, which means that each neuron was sensitive only to light in a particular region of the image;
(b) *bandpass*, in the sense that adding high-frequency components had a negligible effect on the response; and
(c) *oriented*, in that rotating images with sharp edges produced responses only when the edge was within some range of angles.

What's surprising is that if you took a collection of natural images and compressed them by finding a k-dimensional subspace to project them onto using principal component analysis, the directions you find wouldn't have any of these properties. So how are neurons learning the basis they are using to represent images?

What Olshausen and Field [117] proposed was revolutionary. First, what is better about the basis that neurons are using is that they produce sparse activation patterns. Or, in our language, neurons are representing the set of natural images in a basis in which they are sparse. Second, Olshausen and Field proposed that there are natural and biologically plausible rules for learning such a basis. They introduced a simple update rule, whereby neurons that fire together strengthen their connections to each other. This is called a Hebbian learning rule. And empirically, they showed that their iterative algorithm, when run on natural images, recovered a basis that met the above three properties. *Thus algorithms can explain the emergence of certain biological properties of the visual cortex.*

Since then, sparse coding and dictionary learning have become important problems in signal processing and machine learning. We will assume that we are given a collection of examples $b^{(1)}, b^{(2)}, \ldots, b^{(p)}$ that are sparse in a common basis. In particular, there is a matrix A and a set of representations $x^{(1)}, x^{(2)}, \ldots, x^{(p)}$ where $Ax^{(i)} = b^{(i)}$ and each $x^{(i)}$ is sparse. Let's discuss two popular approaches, called the method of optimal directions and k-SVD.

Method of Optimal Directions [68]

Input: Matrix B, whose columns can be jointly sparsely represented
Output: A basis $\widehat{A}$ and representation $\widehat{X}$

Guess $\widehat{A}$

Repeat until convergence:

   Given $\widehat{A}$, compute a column sparse $\widehat{X}$ so that $\widehat{A}\,\widehat{X} \approx B$ (using, e.g., matching pursuit [111] or basis pursuit [50]).

   Given $\widehat{X}$, compute the $\widehat{A}$ that minimizes $\|\widehat{A}\,\widehat{X} - B\|_F$.
End

To simplify our notation, we have organized the observations $b^{(i)}$ as columns in a matrix B and will use the matrix $\widehat{X}$ to represent our estimated sparse representations. Another popular approach is the following:

K-SVD [5]

Input: Matrix B, whose columns can be jointly sparsely represented
Output: A basis $\widehat{A}$ and representation $\widehat{X}$
Guess $\widehat{A}$

Repeat until convergence:

Given $\widehat{A}$, compute a column sparse $\widehat{X}$ so that $\widehat{A}\,\widehat{X} \approx B$ (using, e.g., matching pursuit [111] or basis pursuit [50]).

For each column $\widehat{A}_j$:

Group all samples $b^{(i)}$ where $\widehat{x}^{(i)}$ has a nonzero at index j. Subtract off components in the other directions:

$$b^{(i)} - \sum_{j' \neq j} \widehat{A}_{j'} \widehat{x}^{(i)}_{j'}$$

Organize these vectors into a residual matrix and compute the top singular vector v and update the column $\widehat{A}_j$ to v.

End

You should think about these algorithms as variants of the alternating minimization algorithm we gave for nonnegative matrix factorization. They follow the same style of heuristic. The difference is that k-SVD is more clever about how it corrects for the contribution of the other columns in our basis $\widehat{A}$ when performing an update, which makes it the heuristic of choice in practice. Empirically, both of these algorithms are sensitive to their initialization but work well aside from this issue.

We want algorithms with provable guarantees. Then it is natural to focus on the case where A is a basis for which we know how to solve sparse recovery problems. Thus we could consider both the undercomplete case, where A has full column rank, and the overcomplete case, where there are more columns than rows and A is either incoherent or has the restricted isometry property. That's exactly what we'll do in this chapter. We'll also assume a stochastic model for how the $x^{(i)}$'s are generated, which helps prevent lots of pathologies that can arise (e.g., a column in A is never represented).

6.2 The Undercomplete Case

In this section, we will give an algorithm for sparse coding when A has full column rank. Our approach will be based on a convex programming relaxation and many of the insights that we developed in the previous chapter. We will find our matrix X of sparse representations using the insight that its rows are the sparsest vectors in the row space of our matrix B of samples. More formally, the algorithm of Spielman et al. [131] works under the following natural generative model:

(a) There is an unknown dictionary A that is an $n \times m$ matrix and has full column rank.
(b) Each sample x has independent coordinates, which are nonzero with probability θ. If a coordinate is nonzero, its value is sample from a standard Gaussian.
(c) We observe b where $Ax = b$.

Thus all of our samples are sparse in an unknown basis. So we would like to find A, or equivalently find its left pseudoinverse A^+, which is a linear transformation that makes all of our samples sparse. The parameter θ governs the average sparsity of each representation x and it is required to be neither too big nor too small. More formally, we assume

$$\frac{1}{n} \leq \theta \frac{1}{n^{1/2} \log n}.$$

Spielman et al. [131] gave a polynomial time algorithm to recover A exactly. This is a stronger guarantee than the algorithms we will see later, which merely recover A approximately or to arbitrarily good precision, but require more and more samples to do so. However, the later algorithms will work in the overcomplete case and in the presence of noise. It's also important to note that, strictly speaking, if the coordinates of x_i were independent, we could recover A using algorithms for independent component analysis [74]. However, those algorithms are very sensitive to the independence assumption, and everything we do here will work even under weaker conditions (that are a mouthful to properly spell out).

We will make the simplifying assumption that A is invertible. This doesn't really cost us anything, but let's leave that as an exercise for the reader. In any case, the main insight that underlies the algorithm is contained in the following claims:

Claim 6.2.1 *The row span of B and the row span of $A^{-1}B = X$ are the same.*

Proof: The proof follows by observing that for any vector u,

$$u^T B = (u^T A) A^{-1} B = v^T X.$$

So we can represent any linear combination of the rows of B with a corresponding linear combination of the rows of X. We can obviously go in the reverse direction as well. ∎

We will state the second claim informally for now:

Claim 6.2.2 *Given enough samples, with high probability the sparsest vectors in the row span of X are the rows of X.*

Hopefully this claim is intuitively obvious. The rows of X are independent random vectors whose average sparsity is θ. For our choice of θ, we will have few collisions, which means the sparsity of any two rows of X should be about twice the sparsity of one row.

Now we come to the need for a convex programming relaxation. We can't hope to directly find the sparsest vector in an arbitrary subspace. We proved that that problem is *NP*-hard in Theorem 5.1.5. But let's leverage our insights from sparse recovery and use a convex programming relaxation instead. Consider the following optimization problem:

$$(P_1) \qquad \min \|w^T B\|_1 \text{ s.t. } r^T w = 1$$

This is the usual trick of replacing the sparsity of a vector with its ℓ_1 norm. The constraint $r^T w = 1$ is needed just to fix a normalization, to prevent us from returning the all-zero vector as a solution. We will choose r to be a column in B for reasons that will become clear later. Our goal is to show that the optimal solution to (P_1) is a scaled row of X. In fact, we can transform the above linear program into a simpler one that will be easier to analyze:

$$(Q_1) \qquad \min \|z^T X\|_1 \text{ s.t. } c^T z = 1$$

Lemma 6.2.3 *Let $c = A^{-1} r$. Then there is a bijection between the solutions of (P_1), and the solutions of (Q_1) that preserves the objective value.*

Proof: Given a solution w to (P_1), we can set $z = A^T w$. The objective values are the same because

$$w^T B = w^T A X = z^T X$$

and the linear constraint is met, because again

$$1 = r^T w = r^T (A^T)^{-1} z = r^T (A^{-1})^T z = c^T z$$

and it is easy to check that you can go from a solution to (Q_1) to a solution to (P_1) in the analogous way. ∎

The Minimizers Are Somewhat Sparse

Here we will establish a key step in the analysis. We will show that any optimal solution z_* has its support contained in the support of c. Remember, we chose r to be a column of B. We promised to give an explanation later, so now we can ask: Why did we do this? The point is that if r is a column of B, then the way our bijection between solutions to (P_1) and (Q_1) worked was that we set $c = A^{-1}r$, and so c is a column of X. In our model, c is sparse, so if we show that the support of z_* is contained in the support of c, we'll have proven that z_* is sparse too.

Now let's state and prove the main lemma in this subsection. In what follows, we will assert that certain things happen with high probability but will not dwell on the number of samples needed to make these things be true. Instead, we will give a heuristic argument why the concentration bounds ought to work out that way and focus on the analogy to sparse recovery. For full details, see Spielman et al. [131].

Lemma 6.2.4 *With high probability, any optimal solution z_* to (Q_1) satisfies $supp(z_*) \subseteq supp(c)$.*

Proof: Let's decompose z_* into two parts. Set $J = supp(c)$ and write $z_* = z_0 + z_1$ where z_0 is supported in J and z_1 is supported in $\bar{J}$. Then we have $c^T z_0 = c^T z_*$. What this means is that since z_* is a feasible solution to (Q_1), then z_0 is too. Our goal is to show that z_0 is a strictly better solution to (Q_1) than z_* is. More formally, we want to show:

$$\|z_0^T X\|_1 < \|z_*^T X\|_1.$$

Let S be the set of columns of X that have a nonzero entry in J. That is,

$$S = \{j | X_j^J \neq \vec{0}\}.$$

We now compute:

$$
\begin{aligned}
\|z_*^T X\|_1 &= \|z_*^T X_S\|_1 + \|z_*^T X_{\bar{S}}\|_1 \\
&\geq \|z_0^T X_S\|_1 - \|z_1^T X_S\|_1 + \|z_1^T X_{\bar{S}}\|_1 \\
&\geq \|z_0^T X\|_1 - 2\|z_1^T X_S\|_1 + \|z_1^T X\|_1
\end{aligned}
$$

For now, let's assume the following claim:

Claim 6.2.5 *With high probability, for any nonzero z_1 we have $\|z_1^T X\|_1 > 2\|z_1^T X_S\|_1$.*

With this claim, we have

$$\|z_*^T X\|_1 > \|z_0^T X\|_1$$

which completes the proof. ∎

Now let's prove Claim 6.2.5:

Proof: For now, let's cheat and assume that z_1 is fixed and is a unit vector. Then S is a random set, and if we take p samples from the model we have

$$\mathbb{E}[\|z_1^T X_S\|_1] = \frac{|S|}{p} \mathbb{E}[\|z_1^T X\|_1].$$

The expected size of S is $p \times \mathbb{E}[|\text{supp}(x_i)|] \times \theta = \theta^2 np = o(p)$. Together, these imply that

$$\mathbb{E}[\|z_1^T X\|_1 - 2\|z_1^T X_S\|_1] = \left(1 - \frac{2\,\mathbb{E}[|S|]}{p}\right) \mathbb{E}[\|z_1^T X\|_1]$$

is bounded away from zero, thus proving our desired bound

$$\|z_1^T X\|_1 - 2\|z_1^T X_S\|_1 > 0$$

holds with high probability for any fixed z_1. We can take a union bound over an ϵ-net of all possible unit vectors z_1 and conclude by rescaling that the bound holds for all nonzero z_1's. ∎

The Minimizers Are Rows of X

Now we know that the solutions to (Q_1) are somewhat sparse, because their support is contained in the support of c. But even sparse linear combinations of the rows of X will have few collisions, and so we should expect the ℓ_1 norm to be approximately preserved. More precisely:

Lemma 6.2.6 *With high probability, for any vector z supported in a set J of size at most $10\theta n \log n$, we have*

$$\|z_J^T X^J\|_1 = (1 \pm o(1))C\frac{p}{|J|}\|z_J\|_1$$

where C is the expected absolute value of a nonzero in X.

We will not prove this lemma here. See Spielman et al. [131] for full details. However, the intuition is easy. We should expect most of the columns of X_J to have at most one nonzero element. It is straightforward to analyze the expected contribution of these columns, and the remaining columns have only lower-order contributions. What this means for us is that instead of (Q_1), we can consider

$$(R_1) \qquad \min \|z\|_1 \text{ s.t. } c^T z = 1$$

because the feasible regions of (Q_1) and (R_1) are the same, and their objective value is nearly the same after rescaling. The final step is the following:

Lemma 6.2.7 *If c has a unique coordinate of maximum value c_i, then the unique optimal solution to (R_1) satisfies $z_i = 1/c_i$ and $z_j = 0$ for all other coordinates j.*

Now we can state the main theorem:

Theorem 6.2.8 *[131] Suppose A is an $n \times m$ matrix with full column rank and we are given a polynomial number of samples from the generative model. There is a polynomial time algorithm to recover A exactly (up to a permutation and rescaling of its columns) that succeeds with high probability.*

Proof: The theorem follows by putting together Lemma 6.2.4, Lemma 6.2.6, and Lemma 6.2.7. Using these and the bijection in Lemma 6.2.3, we conclude that for any optimal solution to (P_1), the vector that appears in the objective function is

$$w^T B = z^T X$$

where the only the ith coordinate of z is nonzero. Hence it is a scaled copy of the ith row of X. Now, since the generative model chooses the nonzero entries of x from a standard Gaussian, almost surely there is a coordinate that is the strictly largest in absolute value.

In fact, even more is true. For any fixed coordinate i, with high probability it will be the strictly largest coordinate in absolute value for some column of X. This means that if we repeatedly solve (P_1) by setting r to be different columns of B, then with high probability every row of X will show up. Now, once we know the rows of X, we can solve for A as follows. With high probability, if we take enough samples, then X will have a left pseudo-inverse and we can compute $A = BX^+$, which will recover A up to a permutation and rescaling of its columns. This completes the proof. ∎

6.3 Gradient Descent

Gradient descent and its relatives are some of the most ubiquitous algorithms in machine learning. Traditionally, we are faced with the task of minimizing a convex function $f : \mathbb{R}^n \to \mathbb{R}$ either over all of space (the unconstrained case) or over some convex body K. The simplest possible algorithm you could think of — follow the direction of steepest descent — works. Actually, there are all sorts of convergence guarantees out there, depending on what you know about your function. Is it at least twice differentiable? Do its gradients smoothly vary? Can you fit a quadratic function under it? There are even accelerated methods that get faster rates by leveraging connections to physics, like momentum. You could write an entire book on iterative methods. And indeed there are many terrific sources, such as Nesterov [116] and Rockefellar [127].

In this section we will prove some basic results about gradient descent in the simplest setting, where f is twice differentiable, β-smooth, and α-strongly convex. We will show that the difference between the current value of our objective and the optimal value decays exponentially. Ultimately, our interest in gradient descent will be in applying it to nonconvex problems. Some of the most interesting problems, like fitting parameters in a deep network, are nonconvex. When faced with a nonconvex function f, you just run gradient descent anyway.

It is very challenging to prove guarantees about nonconvex optimization (except for things like being able to reach a local minimum). Nevertheless, our approach for overcomplete sparse coding will be based on an abstraction of the analysis of gradient descent. What is really going on under the hood is that the gradient always points you somewhat in the direction of the globally minimal solution. In nonconvex settings, we will still be able to get some mileage out of this intuition by showing that under the appropriate stochastic assumptions, even simple update rules make progress in a similar manner. In any case, let's now define gradient descent:

Gradient Descent

Given: A convex, differentiable function $f : \mathbb{R}^n \to \mathbb{R}$
Output: A point x_T that is an approximate minimizer of f

For $t = 1$ to T
$\qquad x_{t+1} = x_t - \eta \nabla f(x_t)$
End

The parameter η is called the learning rate. You want to make it large, but not so large that you overshoot. Our analysis of gradient descent will hinge on multivariable calculus. A useful ingredient for us will be the following multivariate Taylor's theorem:

Theorem 6.3.1 *Let $f : \mathbb{R}^n \to \mathbb{R}$ be a convex, differentiable function. Then*

$$f(y) = f(x) + (\nabla f(x))^T (y - x) + \frac{1}{2}(y - x)^T \nabla^2 f(x)(y - x) + o(\|y - x\|^2).$$

Now let's precisely define the conditions on f that we will impose. First we need the gradient to not change too quickly:

Definition 6.3.2 *We will say that f is β-smooth if for all x and y, we have*

$$\|\nabla f(y) - \nabla f(x)\| \le \beta \|y - x\|.$$

Alternatively, if f is twice differentiable, the condition above is equivalent to $\|\nabla^2 f(x)\| \le \beta$ for all x.

Next we need to be able to fit a quadratic function underneath f. We need a condition like this to preclude the case where f is essentially flat for a long time but we need to move far to reach the global minimum. If you can fit a quadratic function underneath f, then you know that the global minimum cannot be too far away from where you currently are.

Definition 6.3.3 *We will say that a convex function f is α-strongly convex if for all x and y, we have*

$$(y - x)^T \nabla^2 f(x)(y - x) \ge \alpha \|y - x\|^2$$

or, equivalently, for all x and y, f satisfies

$$f(y) \ge f(x) + (\nabla f(x))^T (y - x) + \frac{\alpha}{2} \|y - x\|^2.$$

Now let's state the main result we will prove in this section:

Theorem 6.3.4 *Let f be twice differentiable, β-smooth, and α-strongly convex. Let x^* be the minimizer of f and $\eta \le \frac{1}{\beta}$. Then gradient descent starting from x_1 satisfies*

$$f(x_t) - f(x^*) \le \beta \left(1 - \frac{\eta \alpha}{2}\right)^{t-1} \|x_1 - x^*\|^2.$$

We will make use of the following helper lemma:

Lemma 6.3.5 *If f is twice differentiable, β-smooth, and α-strongly convex, then*

$$\nabla f(x_t)^T (x_t - x^*) \ge \frac{\alpha}{4} \|x_t - x^*\|^2 + \frac{1}{2\beta} \|\nabla f(x_t)\|^2.$$

Let's come back to its proof. For now, let's see how it can be used to establish Theorem 6.3.4:

Proof: Let $\alpha' = \frac{\alpha}{4}$ and $\beta' = \frac{1}{2\beta}$. Then we have

$$
\begin{aligned}
\|x_{t+1} - x^*\|^2 &= \|x_t - x^* - \eta \nabla f(x_t)\|^2 \\
&= \|x_t - x^*\|^2 - 2\eta \nabla f(x_t)^T(x_t - x^*) + \eta^2 \|\nabla f(x_t)\|^2 \\
&\leq \|x_t - x^*\|^2 - 2\eta(\alpha' \|x_t - x^*\|^2 + \beta' \|\nabla f(x_t)\|) \\
&= (1 - 2\eta\alpha')\|x_t - x^*\|^2 + (\eta^2 - 2\eta\beta')\|\nabla f(x_t)\|^2 \\
&\leq (1 - 2\eta\alpha')\|x_t - x^*\|^2.
\end{aligned}
$$

The first equality follows from the definition of gradient descent. The first inequality follows from Lemma 6.3.5 and the last inequality from the bound on the learning rate η. To complete the proof, note that

$$
f(x_t) + \nabla f(x_t)^T(x^* - x_t) \leq f(x^*).
$$

Rearranging this inequality and invoking β-smoothness, we have

$$
f(x_t) - f(x^*) \leq \nabla f(x_t)^T(x_t - x^*) \leq \beta \|x_t - x^*\|^2.
$$

And putting it all together, we have

$$
f(x_t) - f(x^*) \leq \beta\left(1 - 2\eta\alpha'\right)\|x_t - x^*\|^2
$$

which completes the proof. ∎

Now let's tie up our loose ends and prove Lemma 6.3.5:

Proof: First, by strong convexity we have

$$
f(x^*) \geq f(x) + \nabla f(x)^T(x^* - x) + \frac{\alpha}{2}\|x - x^*\|^2.
$$

Using the fact that $f(x) \geq f(x^*)$ and rearranging, we get

$$
\nabla f(x)^T(x - x^*) \geq \frac{\alpha}{2}\|x - x^*\|^2.
$$

This is half of the lemma. Now let's relate the left-hand side to the norm of the gradient. Actually, we need a more convenient form of Theorem 6.3.1 that has Lagrange remainder:

Theorem 6.3.6 *Let* $f : \mathbb{R}^n \to \mathbb{R}$ *be a twice differentiable function. Then, for some* $t \in [0, 1]$ *and* $x' = ty + (1 - t)x$, *we have*

$$
\nabla f(x) = \nabla f(y) + \nabla^2 f(x')(x - y).
$$

This can be proven using a multivariate intermediate value theorem. In any case, by setting $y = x^*$ and observing that $\nabla f(x^*) = 0$, we get

$$
\nabla f(x) = \nabla^2 f(x')(x - x^*)
$$

from which we get

$$\nabla f(x)^T (\nabla^2 f(x'))^{-1} \nabla f(x) = \nabla f(x)^T (x - x^*)$$

for some $x' = tx + (1 - t)x^*$. Now, β-smoothness implies that $(\nabla^2 f(x'))^{-1} \geq \frac{1}{\beta} \|\nabla f(x')\|^2$, which gives us

$$\|\nabla f(x)^T (x - x^*)\| \geq \frac{1}{\beta}.$$

Taking the average of the two main inequalities completes the proof. ∎

Actually, our proof works even when the direction you move in is just an approximation to the gradient. This is an important shortcut when, for example, f is a loss function that depends on a very large number of training examples. Instead of computing the gradient of f, you can sample some training examples, compute your loss function on just those, and follow its gradient. This is called *stochastic gradient descent*. The direction it moves in is a random variable whose expectation is the gradient of f. The beauty of it is that the usual proofs of convergence for gradient descent carry over straightforwardly (provided your sample is large enough).

There is an even further abstraction we can make. What if the direction you move in isn't a stochastic approximation of the gradient, but is just some direction that satisfies the conditions shown in Lemma 6.3.5? Let's call this abstract gradient descent, just to give it a name:

Abstract Gradient Descent

Given: A function $f : \mathbb{R}^n \to \mathbb{R}$
Output: A point x_T that is close to x^*

For $t = 1$ to T
    $x_{t+1} = x_t - \eta g_t$
End

Let's introduce the following key definition:

Definition 6.3.7 *We say that g_t is $(\alpha', \beta', \epsilon_t)$-correlated with a point x^* if for all t we have*

$$g_t^T (x_t - x^*) \geq \alpha' \|x_t - x^*\|^2 + \beta' \|g_t\|^2 - \epsilon_t.$$

We have already proven that if f is twice differentiable, β-smooth, and α-strongly convex, then the gradient is $(\frac{\alpha}{4}, \frac{1}{2\beta}, 0)$-correlated with the optimal solution x^*. It turns out that the proof we gave of Theorem 6.3.4 generalizes immediately to this more abstract setting:

Theorem 6.3.8 *Suppose that g_t is $(\alpha', \beta', \epsilon_t)$-correlated with a point x^* and, moreover, $\eta \leq 2\beta'$. Then abstract gradient descent starting from x_1 satisfies*

$$\|x_t - x^*\|^2 \leq \left(1 - \frac{\eta\alpha'}{2}\right)^{t-1} \|x_1 - x^*\|^2 + \frac{\max_t \epsilon_t}{\alpha'}.$$

Now we have the tools we need for overcomplete sparse coding. We'll prove convergence bounds for iterative methods in spite of the fact that the underlying function they are attempting to minimize is nonconvex. The key is to use the above framework and exploit the stochastic properties of our model.

6.4 The Overcomplete Case

In this section, we will give an algorithm for sparse coding that works for overcomplete dictionaries. As usual, we will work in a stochastic model. More formally, x is a random k-sparse vector generated according to the following procedure:

(a) The support of x is chosen uniformly at random from all size k subsets of $[m]$.
(b) If the jth coordinate is nonzero, then its value is independently chosen to be $+1$ or -1 (with equal probability).

And we observe just the right-hand side of $Ax = b$. Our goal is to learn the columns of A given enough samples from the model. Actually, we've made some simplifying assumptions in the above model that we won't actually need. We don't really need the support of x to be chosen uniformly at random, or the coordinates to be independent. In fact, our algorithms will even be able to tolerate additive noise. Nevertheless, our model is easier to think about, so let's stick with it.

Now we come to the main conceptual insight. Usually we think of iterative algorithms as performing alternating minimization on a nonconvex objective function. For example, a popular energy function in the context of sparse coding is the following:

$$\mathcal{E}(\widehat{A}, \widehat{X}) = \sum_{i=1}^{p} \|b^{(i)} - \widehat{A}\widehat{x}^{(i)}\|^2 + \sum_{i=1}^{p} L(\widehat{x}^{(i)})$$

where $Ax^{(i)} = b^{(i)}$ are our observed samples. Moreover, L is a loss function that penalizes for vectors $\widehat{x}^{(i)}$ that are not k-sparse. You can think of this as being a hard penalty function that is infinite when x has more than k nonzero coordinates and is zero otherwise. It could also be your favorite sparsity-inducing soft penalty function.

Many iterative algorithms attempt to minimize an energy function like the one above that balances how well your basis explains each sample and how sparse each representation is. The trouble is that the function is nonconvex, so if you want to give provable guarantees, you would have to figure out all kinds of things, like why it doesn't get stuck in a local minimum or why it doesn't spend too much time moving slowly around saddle points.

Question 8 *Instead of viewing iterative methods as attempting to minimize a known nonconvex function, can we view them as minimizing an unknown convex function?*

What we mean is: What if, instead of the $\widehat{x}$'s, we plug in the true sparse representations x? Our energy function becomes

$$\mathcal{E}(\widehat{A}, X) = \sum_{i=1}^{p} \|b^{(i)} - \widehat{A} x^{(i)}\|^2$$

which is convex, because only the basis A is unknown. Moreover, it's natural to expect that in our stochastic model (and probably many others), the minimizer of $\mathcal{E}(\widehat{A}, X)$ converges to the true basis A. So now we have a convex function where there is a path from our initial solution to the optimal solution via gradient descent. The trouble is that we cannot evaluate or compute gradients of the function $\mathcal{E}(\widehat{A}, X)$, because X is unknown.

The path we will follow in this section is to show that simple, iterative algorithms for sparse coding move in a direction that is an approximation to the gradient of $\mathcal{E}(\widehat{A}, X)$. More precisely, we will show that under our stochastic model, the direction our update rule moves in meets the conditions in Definition 6.3.7. That's our plan of action. We will study the following iterative algorithm:

Hebbian Rule for Sparse Coding

Input: Samples $b = Ax$ and an estimate $\widehat{A}$
Output: An improved estimate $\widehat{A}$

For $t = 0$ to T

    Decode using the current dictionary:

$$\widehat{x}^{(i)} = \text{threshold}_{1/2}(\widehat{A}^T b^{(i)})$$

Update the dictionary:

$$\widehat{A} \leftarrow \widehat{A} + \eta \sum_{i=qt+1}^{q(t+1)} (b^{(i)} - \widehat{A}\widehat{x}^{(i)}) \, \text{sign}(\widehat{x}^{(i)})^T$$

End

We have used the following notation:

Definition 6.4.1 *Let* sign *denote the entrywise operation that sets positive coordinates to* $+1$, *negative coordinates to* -1, *and zero to zero. Also, let* threshold$_C$ *denote the entrywise operation that zeros out coordinates whose absolute value is less than* $C/2$ *and keeps the rest of the coordinates the same.*

The update rule is also natural in another sense. In the context of neuroscience, the dictionary A often represents the connection weights between two adjacent layers of neurons. Then the update rule has the property that it strengthens the connections between pairs of neurons that fire together when you set up a neural network that computes the sparse representation. Recall, these are called *Hebbian* rules.

Now let's define the metric we will use to measure how close our estimate $\widehat{A}$ is to the true dictionary A. As usual, we cannot hope to recover which column is which or the correct sign, so we need to take this into account:

Definition 6.4.2 *We will say that two* $n \times m$ *matrices* $\widehat{A}$ *and* A, *whose columns are unit vectors, are* (δ, κ)-*close if there is a permutation and sign flip of the columns of* $\widehat{A}$ *that results in a matrix* B *that satisifes*

$$\|B_i - A_i\| \le \delta$$

for all i, *and furthermore* $\|B - A\| \le \kappa \|A\|$.

First let's analyze the decoding step of the algorithm:

Lemma 6.4.3 *Suppose that* A *is an* $n \times m$ *matrix that is* μ-*incoherent and that* $Ax = b$ *is generated from the stochastic model. Further suppose that*

$$k \le \frac{1}{10\mu \log n}$$

and $\widehat{A}$ *is* $(1/\log n, 2)$-*close to* A. *Then decoding succeeds; i.e.,*

$$\text{sign}(\text{threshold}_{1/2}(\widehat{A}^T b)) = \text{sign}(x)$$

with high probability.

We will not prove this lemma here. The idea is that for any j, we can write

$$(\widehat{A}^T b)_j = A_j^T A_j x_j + (\widehat{A}_j - A_j)^T A_j x_j + \widehat{A}_j^T \sum_{i \in S \setminus \{j\}} A_i x_i$$

where $S = \text{supp}(x)$. The first term is x_j. The second term is at most $1/\log n$ in absolute value. And the third term is a random variable whose variance can be appropriately bounded. For the full details, see Arora et al. [16]. Keep in mind that for incoherent dictionaries, we think of $\mu = 1/\sqrt{n}$.

Let γ denote any vector whose norm is negligible (say $n^{-\omega(1)}$). We will use γ to collect various sorts of error terms that are small, without having to worry about what the final expression looks like. Consider the expected direction that our Hebbian update moves in when restricted to some column j. We have

$$g_j = \mathbb{E}[(b - \widehat{A}\widehat{x})\,\text{sign}(\widehat{x}_j)]$$

where the expectation is over a sample $Ax = b$ from our model. This is a priori a complicated expression to analyze, because b is a random variable of our model and $\widehat{x}$ is a random variable that arises from our decoding rule. Our main lemma is the following:

Lemma 6.4.4 *Suppose that $\widehat{A}$ and A are $(1/\log n, 2)$-close. Then*

$$g_j = p_j q_j (I - \widehat{A}_j \widehat{A}_j^T) A_j + p_j \widehat{A}_{-j} Q \widehat{A}_{-j}^T A_j \pm \gamma$$

where $q_j = \mathbb{P}[j \in S]$, $q_{i,j} = \mathbb{P}[i, j \in S]$ and $p_j = \mathbb{E}[x_j \text{sign}(x_j) | j \in S]$. Moreover, $Q = \text{diag}(\{q_{i,j}\}_i)$.

Proof: Using the fact that the decoding step recovers the correct signs of x with high probability, we can play various tricks with the indicator variable for whether or not the decoding succeeds and be able to replace $\widehat{x}$'s with x's. For now, let's state the following claim, which we will prove later:

Claim 6.4.5 $g_j = \mathbb{E}[(I - \widehat{A}_S \widehat{A}_S^T) Ax\, sign(x_j))] \pm \gamma$

Now let $S = \text{supp}(x)$. We will imagine first sampling the support of x, then choosing the values of its nonzero entries. Thus we can rewrite the expectation using subconditioning as

$$g_j = \mathbb{E}_{S}[\mathbb{E}_{x_S}[(I - \widehat{A}_S \widehat{A}_S^T) Ax\, \text{sign}(x_j))] | S] \pm \gamma$$

$$= \mathbb{E}_{S}[\mathbb{E}_{x_S}[(I - \widehat{A}_S \widehat{A}_S^T) A_j x_j\, \text{sign}(x_j))] | S] \pm \gamma$$

$$= p_j \mathbb{E}_{S}[(I - \widehat{A}_S \widehat{A}_S^T) A_j] \pm \gamma$$

$$= p_j q_j (I - \widehat{A}_j \widehat{A}_j^T) A_j + p_j \widehat{A}_{-j} Q \widehat{A}_{-j}^T A_j \pm \gamma.$$

The second equality uses the fact that the coordinates are uncorrelated, conditioned on the support S. The third equality uses the definition of p_j. The fourth equality follows from separating the contribution from j from all the other coordinates, where A_{-j} denotes the matrix we obtain by deleting the jth column. This now completes the proof of the main lemma. ∎

So why does this lemma tell us that our update rule meets the conditions in Definition 6.3.7? When $\widehat{A}$ and A are close, you should think of the expression as follows:

$$g_j = \underbrace{p_j q_j (I - \widehat{A}_j \widehat{A}_j^T) A_j}_{\approx p_j q_j (A_j - \widehat{A}_j)} + \underbrace{p_j \widehat{A}_{-j} Q \widehat{A}_{-j}^T A_j}_{\text{systemic error}} \pm \gamma$$

And so the expected direction that the update rule moves in is almost the ideal direction $A_j - \widehat{A}_j$, pointing toward the true solution. What this tells us is that sometimes the way to get around nonconvexity is to have a reasonable stochastic model. Even though in a worst-case sense you can still get stuck in a local minimum, in the average case you often make progress with each step you take. We have not discussed the issue of how to initialize it. But it turns out that there are simple spectral algorithms to find a good initialization. See Arora et al. [16] for the full details, as well as the guarantees of the overall algorithm.

Let's conclude by proving Claim 6.4.5:

Proof: Let F denote the event that decoding recovers the correct signs of x. From Lemma 6.4.3, we know that F holds with high probability. First let's use the indicator variable for event F to replace the $\widehat{x}$ inside the sign function with x at the expense of adding a negligible error term:

$$g_j = \mathbb{E}[(b - \widehat{A}x) \, \text{sign}(\widehat{x}_j) \mathbb{1}_F] + \mathbb{E}[(b - \widehat{A}x) \, \text{sign}(\widehat{x}_j) \mathbb{1}_{\overline{F}}]$$
$$= \mathbb{E}[(b - \widehat{A}x) \, \text{sign}(x_j) \mathbb{1}_F] \pm \gamma$$

The equality uses the fact that $\text{sign}(\widehat{x}_j) = \text{sign}(x_j)$ when event F occurs. Now let's substitute in for $\widehat{x}$:

$$g_j = \mathbb{E}[(b - \widehat{A} \, \text{threshold}_{1/2}(\widehat{A}^T b)) \, \text{sign}(x_j) \mathbb{1}_F] \pm \gamma$$
$$= \mathbb{E}[(b - \widehat{A}_S \widehat{A}_S^T b) \, \text{sign}(x_j) \mathbb{1}_F] \pm \gamma$$
$$= \mathbb{E}[(I - \widehat{A}_S \widehat{A}_S^T) b \, \text{sign}(x_j) \mathbb{1}_F] \pm \gamma$$

Here we have used the fact that $\text{threshold}_{1/2}(\widehat{A}^T b)$ keeps all coordinates in S the same and zeros out the rest when event F occurs. Now we can play some more tricks with the indicator variable to get rid of it:

$$g_j = \mathbb{E}[(I - \widehat{A_S}\widehat{A_S^T})b \operatorname{sign}(x_j)] - \mathbb{E}[(I - \widehat{A_S}\widehat{A_S^T})b \operatorname{sign}(x_j)\mathbb{1}_{\overline{F}}] \pm \gamma$$
$$= \mathbb{E}[(I - \widehat{A_S}\widehat{A_S^T})b \operatorname{sign}(x_j)] \pm \gamma$$

which completes the proof of the claim. Line by line, the manipulations are trivial, but they yield a useful expression for the update rule. ∎

There are other, earlier algorithms for overcomplete sparse coding. Arora et al. [15] gave an algorithm based on overlapping clustering that works for incoherent dictionaries almost up to the threshold where the sparse recovery problem has a unique solution, a la Lemma 5.2.3. Agarwal et al. [2, 3] gave algorithms for overcomplete, incoherent dictionaries that work up to thresholds that are worse by a polynomial factor. Barak et al. [25] gave algorithms based on the sum-of-squares hierarchy that work with nearly linear sparsity, but where the degree of the polynomial depends on the desired accuracy.

6.5 Exercises

Problem 6-1: Consider the sparse coding model $y = Ax$ where A is a fixed $n \times n$ matrix with orthonormal columns a_i, and x has i.i.d. coordinates drawn from the distribution

$$x_i = \begin{cases} +1 & \text{with probability } \alpha/2, \\ -1 & \text{with probability } \alpha/2, \\ 0 & \text{with probability } 1 - \alpha. \end{cases}$$

The goal is to recover the columns of A (up to sign and permutation) given many independent samples y. Construct the matrix

$$M = \mathbb{E}_y\left[\langle y^{(1)}, y \rangle \langle y^{(2)}, y \rangle y y^T \right]$$

where $y^{(1)} = Ax^{(1)}$ and $y^{(2)} = Ax^{(2)}$ are two fixed samples from the sparse coding model, and the expectation is over a third sample y from the sparse coding model. Let $\hat{z}$ be the (unit-norm) eigenvector of M corresponding to the largest (in absolute value) eigenvalue.

(a) Write an expression for M in terms of $\alpha, x^{(1)}, x^{(2)}, \{a_i\}$.
(b) Assume for simplicity that $x^{(1)}$ and $x^{(2)}$ both have support size exactly αn and that their supports intersect at a single coordinate i^*. Show that $\langle \hat{z}, a_{i^*} \rangle^2 \geq 1 - O(\alpha^2 n)$ in the limit $\alpha \to 0$.

This method can be used to find a good starting point for alternating minimization.

7

Gaussian Mixture Models

Many natural statistics, such as the distribution of people's heights, can be modeled as a mixture of Gaussians. The components of the mixture represent the parts of the distribution coming from different subpopulations. But if we don't know about the subpopulations in advance, can we figure out what they are and learn their parameters? And can we then classify samples based on which subpopulation they are likely to have come from? In this chapter we will give the first algorithms for learning the parameters of a mixture of Gaussians at an inverse polynomial rate. The one-dimensional case was introduced by Karl Pearson, who was one of the founders of statistics. We will show the first provable guarantees for his method. Building on this, we will solve the high-dimensional learning problem too. Along the way, we will develop insights about systems of polynomial equations and how they can be used for parameter learning.

7.1 Introduction

Karl Pearson was one of the luminaries of statistics and helped to lay its foundation. He introduced revolutionary new ideas and methods, such as:

(a) p-values, which are now the de facto way to measure statistical significance
(b) The chi-squared test, which measures goodness of fit to a Gaussian distribution
(c) Pearson's correlation coefficient
(d) The method of moments for estimating the parameters of a distribution
(e) Mixture models for modeling the presence of subpopulations

Believe it or not, the last two were introduced in the same influential study from 1894 that represented Pearson's first foray into biometrics [120]. Let's understand what led Pearson down this road. While on vacation, his colleague Walter Weldon and his wife had meticulously collected 1,000 Naples crabs and measured 23 different physical attributes of each of them. But there was a surprise lurking in the data. All but one of these statistics was approximately Gaussian. So why weren't they all Gaussian?

Everyone was quite puzzled, until Pearson offered an explanation: *Maybe the Naples crab is not one species, but rather two species.* Then it is natural to model the observed distribution as a mixture of two Gaussians, rather than just one. Let's be more formal. Recall that the density function of a one-dimensional Gaussian with mean μ and variance σ^2 is

$$\mathcal{N}(\mu, \sigma^2, x) = \frac{1}{\sqrt{2\pi\sigma^2}} exp \left\{ \frac{-(x-\mu)^2}{2\sigma^2} \right\}.$$

And for a mixture of two Gaussians, it is

$$F(x) = w_1 \underbrace{\mathcal{N}(\mu_1, \sigma_1^2, x)}_{F_1(x)} + (1 - w_1) \underbrace{\mathcal{N}(\mu_2, \sigma_2^2, x)}_{F_2(x)}.$$

We will use F_1 and F_2 to denote the two Gaussians in the mixture. You can also think of it in terms of how you'd generate a sample from it: Take a biased coin that is heads with probability w_1 and tails with the remaining probability $1-w_1$. Then for each sample you flip the coin; i.e., decide which subpopulation your sample comes from. If it's heads, you output a sample from the first Gaussian, otherwise you output a sample from the second one.

This is already a powerful and flexible statistical model (see Figure 7.1). But Pearson didn't stop there. He wanted to find the parameters of a mixture of two Gaussians that best fit the observed data to test out his hypothesis. When it's just one Gaussian, it's easy, because you can set μ and σ^2 to be the empirical mean and empirical variance, respectively. But what should you do when there are five unknown parameters and for each sample there is a hidden variable representing which subpopulation it came from? Pearson used the method of moments, which we will explain in the next subsection. The parameters he found seemed to be a good fit, but there were still a lot of unanswered questions, such as: Does the method of moments always find a good solution if there is one?

Method of Moments

Here we will explain how Pearson used the method of moments to find the unknown parameters. The key observation is that the moments of a mixture

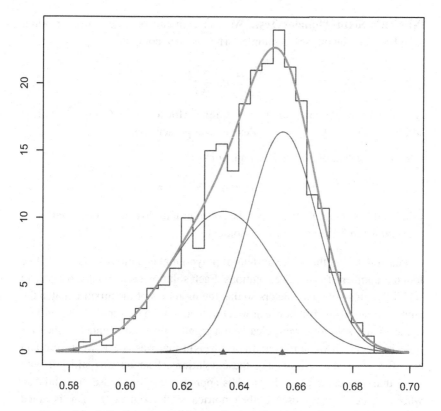

Figure 7.1: A fit of a mixture of two univariate Gaussians to Pearson's data on Naples crabs, created by Peter Macdonald using R.

of Gaussians are themselves polynomials in the unknown parameters. Let's denote the rth raw moments of a Gaussian by M_r:

$$\underset{x \leftarrow F_1(x)}{\mathbb{E}} \left[x^r \right] = M_r(\mu, \sigma)$$

It is easy to compute $M_1(\mu, \sigma) = \mu$ and $M_2(\mu, \sigma) = \mu^2 + \sigma^2$, etc., and check that M_r is a degree r polynomial in μ and σ. Now we have

$$\underset{x \leftarrow F(x)}{\mathbb{E}} \left[x^r \right] = w_1 M_r(\mu_1, \sigma_1) + (1 - w_1)M_r(\mu_2, \sigma_2) = P_r(w_1, \mu_1, \sigma_1, \mu_2, \sigma_2).$$

And so the rth raw moment of a mixture of two Gaussians is itself a degree $r + 1$ polynomial, which we denote by P_r, in the parameters we would like to learn.

Pearson's Sixth Moment Test: We can estimate $\mathbb{E}_{x \leftarrow F}[x^r]$ from random samples. Let S be our set of samples. Then we can compute:

$$\widetilde{M}_r = \frac{1}{|S|} \sum_{x \in S} x^r$$

And given a polynomial number of samples (for any $r = O(1)$), $\widetilde{M}_r$ will be additively close to $\mathbb{E}_{x \leftarrow F(x)}[x^r]$. Pearson's approach was:

- Set up a system of polynomial equations

$$\Big\{ P_r(w_1, \mu_1, \sigma_1, \mu_2, \sigma_2) = \widetilde{M}_r \Big\}, \ r = 1, 2, \ldots, 5.$$

- Solve this system. Each solution is a setting of all five parameters that explains the first five empirical moments.

Pearson solved the above system of polynomial equations *by hand*, and he found a number of candidate solutions. Each solution corresponds to a way to set all five unknown parameters so that the moments of the mixture match the empirical moments. But how can we choose among these candidate solutions? Some of the solutions were clearly not right; some had negative values for the variance, or a value for the mixing weight that was not between zero and one. But even after eliminating these solutions, Pearson was still left with more than one candidate solution. His approach was to choose the candidate whose prediction was closest to the empirical sixth moment $\widetilde{M}_6$. This is called the *sixth moment test*.

Expectation Maximization

The workhorse in modern statistics is the *maximum likelihood estimator*, which sets the parameters so as to maximize the probability that the mixture would generate the observed samples. This estimator has lots of wonderful properties. Under certain technical conditions, it is *asymptotically efficient*, meaning that no other estimator can achieve asymptotically smaller variance as a function of the number of samples. Even the law of its distribution can be characterized, and is known to be normally distributed with a variance related to what's called the Fisher information. Unfortunately, for most of the problems we will be interested in, it is *NP*-hard to compute [19].

The popular alternative is known as *expectation maximization* and was introduced in an influential paper by Dempster, Laird, and Rubin [61]. It is important to realize that this is just a heuristic for computing the maximum likelihood estimator and does not inherit any of its statistical guarantees.

Expectation maximization is a general approach for dealing with latent variables where we alternate between estimating the latent variables given our current set of parameters, and updating our parameters. In the case of mixtures of two Gaussians, it repeats the following until convergence:

- For each $x \in S$, calculate the posterior probability:

$$\widehat{w}_1(x) = \frac{\widehat{w}_1 \widehat{F}_1(x)}{\widehat{w}_1 \widehat{F}_1(x) + (1 - \widehat{w}_1)\widehat{F}_2(x)}$$

- Update the mixing weights:

$$\widehat{w}_1 \leftarrow \frac{\sum_{x \in S} \widehat{w}_1(x)}{|S|}$$

- Reestimate the parameters:

$$\widehat{\mu}_i \leftarrow \frac{\sum_{x \in S} \widehat{w}_i(x)x}{\sum_{x \in S} \widehat{w}_i(x)}, \quad \widehat{\Sigma}_i \leftarrow \frac{\sum_{x \in S} \widehat{w}_i(x)(x - \widehat{\mu}_i)(x - \widehat{\mu}_i)^T}{\sum_{x \in S} \widehat{w}_i(x)}$$

In practice, it seems to work well. But it can get stuck in local maxima of the likelihood function. Even worse, it can be quite sensitive to how it is initialized (see, e.g., [125]).

7.2 Clustering-Based Algorithms

Our basic goal will be to give algorithms that provably compute the true parameters of a mixture of Gaussians, given a polynomial number of random samples. This question was introduced in the seminal paper of Dasgupta [56], and the first generation of algorithms focused on the high-dimensional case where the components are far enough apart that they have essentially no *overlap*. The next generation of algorithms are based on algebraic insights and avoid clustering altogether.

The High-Dimensional Geometry of Gaussians

Before we proceed, we will discuss some of the counterintuitive properties of high-dimensional Gaussians. First, the density of a multidimensional Gaussian in $\mathbb{R}^n$ is given by

$$\mathcal{N}(\mu, \Sigma) = \frac{1}{(2\pi)^{n/2} det(\Sigma)^{1/2}} exp \left\{ \frac{-(x - \mu)^T \Sigma^{-1}(x - \mu)}{2} \right\}.$$

Here, Σ is the covariance matrix. If $\Sigma = \sigma^2 I_n$ and $\mu = \vec{0}$, then the distribution is just $\mathcal{N}(0, \sigma^2) \times \mathcal{N}(0, \sigma^2) \times \ldots \times \mathcal{N}(0, \sigma^2)$ and we call it a spherical Gaussian, because the density function is rotationally invariant.

Fact 7.2.1 *The maximum value of the density function is at $x = \mu$.*

Fact 7.2.2 *For a spherical Gaussian, almost all the weight of the density function has $\|x - \mu\|_2^2 = \sigma^2 n \pm \sigma^2 \sqrt{n \log n}$.*

At first, these facts might seem to be inconsistent. The first one tells us that the most probable value of a sample is at zero. The second one tells us that almost all of the samples are far from zero. It's easiest to think about what's happening in spherical coordinates. The maximum of the density function is when the radius $R = 0$. But the rate at which the surface area of the sphere increases is much faster than the rate that the density function decreases, until we reach a radius of $R = \sigma\sqrt{n}$. Really, we should think about a high-dimensional spherical Gaussian as being essentially a thin spherical shell.

The Cluster-Then-Learn Paradigm

Clustering-based algorithms are all based on the following strategy:

- Cluster all of the samples S into two sets S_1 and S_2 depending on whether they were generated by the first or second component.
- Output the empirical mean and covariance of each S_i along with the empirical mixing weight $\frac{|S_1|}{|S|}$.

The details of how we will implement the first step and what types of conditions we need to impose will vary from algorithm to algorithm. But first let's see that if we could design a clustering algorithm that succeeds with high probability, the parameters we find would be provably good estimates for the true ones. This is captured by the following lemmas. Let $|S| = m$ be the number of samples.

Lemma 7.2.3 *If $m \geq C \frac{\log 1/\delta}{\epsilon^2}$ and clustering succeeds, then*

$$|\widehat{w}_1 - w_1| \leq \epsilon$$

with probability at least $1 - \delta$.

Now let $w_{min} = \min(w_1, 1 - w_1)$. Then

Lemma 7.2.4 *If $m \geq C \frac{n \log 1/\delta}{w_{min} \epsilon^2}$ and clustering succeeds, then*

$$\|\widehat{\mu}_i - \mu_i\|_2 \leq \epsilon$$

for each i, with probability at least $1 - \delta$.

Finally, let's show that the empirical covariance is close too:

Lemma 7.2.5 *If* $m \geq C \frac{n \log 1/\delta}{w_{min}\epsilon^2}$ *and clustering succeeds, then*

$$\|\widehat{\Sigma}_i - \Sigma_i\| \leq \epsilon$$

for each i, with probability at least $1 - \delta$.

All of these lemmas can be proven via standard concentration bounds. The first two follow from concentration bounds for scalar random variables, and the third requires more high-powered matrix concentration bounds. However, it is easy to prove a version of this that has a worse but still polynomial dependence on n by proving that each entry of $\widehat{\Sigma}_i$ and Σ_i are close and using the union bound. What these lemmas together tell us is that if we really could solve clustering, then we would indeed be able to provably estimate the unknown parameters.

Dasgupta [56]: $\widetilde{\Omega}(\sqrt{n})$ Separation

Dasgupta gave the first provable algorithms for learning mixtures of Gaussians, and required that $\|\mu_i - \mu_j\|_2 \geq \widetilde{\Omega}(\sqrt{n}\sigma_{max})$ where σ_{max} is the maximum variance of any Gaussian in any direction (e.g., if the components are not spherical). Note that the constant in the separation depends on w_{min}, and we assume we know this parameter (or a lower bound on it).

The basic idea behind the algorithm is to project the mixture onto $\log k$ dimensions uniformly at random. This projection will preserve distances between each pair of centers μ_i and μ_j with high probability, but will contract distances between samples from the same component and make each component closer to spherical, thus making it easier to cluster. Informally, we can think of this separation condition as: if we think of each Gaussian as a spherical ball, then if the components are far enough apart, these balls will be *disjoint*.

Arora and Kannan [19] and Dasgupta and Schulman [64]: $\widetilde{\Omega}(n^{1/4})$ Separation

We will describe the approach in [19] in detail. The basic question is, if $\sqrt{n}$ separation is the threshold where we can think of the components as disjoint, how can we learn when the components are much closer? In fact, even if the components are only $\widetilde{\Omega}(n^{1/4})$ separated, it is still true that *every* pair of samples from the same component is closer than *every* pair of samples from different components. How can this be? The explanation is that even though the balls representing each component are no longer disjoint, we are still very unlikely to sample from their overlap region.

Consider $x, x' \leftarrow F_1$, and $y \leftarrow F_2$.

Claim 7.2.6 *All of the vectors* $x - \mu_1, x' - \mu_1, \mu_1 - \mu_2, y - \mu_2$ *are nearly orthogonal (whp).*

This claim is immediate, since the vectors $x - \mu_1, x' - \mu_1, y - \mu_2$ are uniform from a sphere, and $\mu_1 - \mu_2$ is the only fixed vector. In fact, any set of vectors in which all but one are uniformly random from a sphere are nearly orthogonal.

Now we can compute:

$$\|x - x'\|^2 \approx \|x - \mu_1\|^2 + \|\mu_1 - x'\|^2$$
$$\approx 2n\sigma^2 \pm 2\sigma^2 \sqrt{n \log n}$$

And similarly:

$$\|x - y\|^2 \approx \|x - \mu_1\|^2 + \|\mu_1 - \mu_2\|^2 + \|\mu_2 - y\|^2$$
$$\approx 2n\sigma^2 + \|\mu_1 - \mu_2\|^2 \pm 2\sigma^2 \sqrt{n \log n}$$

Hence if $\|\mu_1 - \mu_2\| = \widetilde{\Omega}(n^{1/4}, \sigma)$, then $\|\mu_1 - \mu_2\|^2$ is larger than the error term and each pair of samples from the same component will be closer than each pair from different components. Indeed, we can find the right threshold τ and correctly cluster all of the samples. Again, we can output the empirical mean, empirical covariance, and relative size of each cluster, and these will be good estimates of the true parameters.

Vempala and Wang [141]: $\widetilde{\Omega}(k^{1/4})$ Separation

Vempala and Wang [141] removed the dependence on n and replaced it with a separation condition that depends on k, the number of components. The idea is that if we could project the mixture into the subspace T spanned by $\{\mu_1, \ldots, \mu_k\}$, we would preserve the separation between each pair of components but reduce the ambient dimension.

So how can we find T, the subspace spanned by the means? We will restrict our discussion to a mixture of spherical Gaussians with a common variance $\sigma^2 I$. Let $x \sim F$ be a random sample from the mixture; then we can write $x = c + z$ where $z \sim N(0, \sigma^2 I_n)$ and c is a random vector that takes the value μ_i with probability w_i for each $i \in [k]$. So:

$$\mathbb{E}[xx^T] = \mathbb{E}[cc^T] + \mathbb{E}[zz^T] = \sum_{i=1}^{k} w_i \mu_i \mu_i^T + \sigma^2 I_n$$

Hence the top left singular vectors of $\mathbb{E}[xx^T]$, whose singular value is strictly larger than σ^2, exactly span T. We can then estimate $\mathbb{E}[xx^T]$ from sufficiently many random samples, compute its singular value decomposition, and project the mixture onto T and invoke the algorithm of [19].

Brubaker and Vempala [40]: Separating Hyperplane

What if the largest variance of any component is much larger than the separation between the components? Brubaker and Vempala [40] observed that none of the existing algorithms succeed for a mixture that looks like a pair of *parallel pancakes*. In this example, there is a hyperplane that separates the mixture so that almost all of one component is on one side and almost all of the other component is on the other side. They gave an algorithm that succeeds, provided that such a separating hyperplane exists; however, the conditions are more complex to state for mixtures of three or more Gaussians. With three components, it is easy to construct mixtures that we can hope to learn, but where there are no hyperplanes that separate one component from the others.

7.3 Discussion of Density Estimation

The algorithms we have discussed so far all rely on clustering. But there are some cases where this strategy just won't work, because clustering is information theoretically impossible. More precisely, we will show that if $d_{TV}(F_1, F_2) = 1/2$, then we will quickly encounter a sample where we cannot figure out which component generated it, even if we know the true parameters.

Let's formalize this through the notion of a coupling:

Definition 7.3.1 *A coupling between F and G is a distribution on pairs (x, y) so that the marginal distribution on x is F and the marginal distribution on y is G. The error is the probability that $x \neq y$.*

So what is the error of the best coupling? It is easy to see that it is exactly the total variation distance:

Claim 7.3.2 *There is a coupling with error ε between F and G if and only if $d_{TV}(F, G) \leq \varepsilon$.*

In fact, this is a nice way to think about the total variation distance. Operationally upper-bounding the total variation distance tells us there is a good coupling. In a similar manner, you can interpret the KL divergence as the penalty you pay (in terms of expected coding length) when you optimally encode samples from one distribution using the best code for the other.

Returning to the problem of clustering the samples from a mixture of two Gaussians, suppose we have $d_{TV}(F_1, F_2) = 1/2$ and that

$$F(x) + 1/2F_1(x) + 1/2F_2(x).$$

Using the above claim, we know that there is a coupling between F_1 and F_2 that agrees with probability $1/2$. Hence, instead of thinking about sampling from a mixture of two Gaussians in the usual way (choose which component, then choose a random sample from it), we can alternatively sample as follows:

1. Choose (x, y) from the best coupling between F_1 and F_2.
2. If $x = y$, output x with probability $1/2$, and otherwise output y.
3. Else output x with probability $1/2$, and otherwise output y.

This procedure generates a random sample from F just as before. What's important is that if you reach the second step, the value you output doesn't depend on which component the sample came from. So you can't predict it better than randomly guessing. This is a useful way to think about the assumptions that clustering-based algorithms make. Some are stronger than others, but at the very least they need to take at least n samples and cluster all of them correctly. In order for this to be possible, we must have

$$d_{TV}(F_1, F_2) \geq 1 - 1/n.$$

But who says that algorithms for learning must first cluster? Can we hope to learn the parameters even when the components almost entirely overlap, such as when $d_{TV}(F_1, F_2) = 1/n$?

Now is a good time to discuss the types of goals we could aim for and how they relate to each other.

(a) Improper Density Estimation

This is the weakest learning goal. If we're given samples from some distribution F in some class $\mathcal{C}$ (e.g., $\mathcal{C}$ could be all mixtures of two Gaussians), then we want to find any other distribution $\widehat{F}$ that satisfies $d_{TV}(F, \widehat{F}) \leq \varepsilon$. We do not require $\widehat{F}$ to be in class $\mathcal{C}$ too. What's important to know about improper density estimation is that in one dimension it's easy. You can solve it using a kernel density estimate, provided that F is smooth.

Here's how kernel density estimates work. First you take many samples and construct an empirical point mass distribution G. Now, G is not close to F. It's not even smooth, so how can it be? But you can fix this by convolving with a Gaussian with small variance. In particular, if you set $\widehat{F} = G * \mathcal{N}(0, \sigma^2)$ and choose the parameters and number of samples appropriately, what you get will satisfy $d_{TV}(F, \widehat{F}) \leq \varepsilon$ with high probability. This scheme doesn't use much about the distribution F, but it pays the price in high dimensions. The issue is that you just won't get enough samples that are close to each other. In general, kernel density estimates need the number of samples to be exponential in the dimension in order to work.

(b) **Proper Density Estimation**

Proper density estimation is the same but stronger, in that it requires $\widehat{F} \in \mathcal{C}$. Sometimes you can interpolate between improper and proper density estimation by constraining $\widehat{F}$ to be in some larger class that contains $\mathcal{C}$. It's also worth noting that sometimes you can just take a kernel density estimate or anything else that solves the improper density estimation problem and look for the $\widehat{F} \in \mathcal{C}$ that is closest to your improper estimate. This would definitely work, but the trouble is that algorithmically, it's usually not clear how to find the closest distribution in some class to some other unwieldy target distribution. Finally, we reach the strongest type of goal:

(c) **Parameter Learning**

Here we not only require that $d_{TV}(F, \widehat{F}) \leq \varepsilon$ and that $\widehat{F} \in \mathcal{C}$, but we want $\widehat{F}$ to be a good estimate for F *on a component-by-component basis*. For example, our goal specialized to the case of mixtures of two Gaussians is:

Definition 7.3.3 *We will say that a mixture* $\widehat{F} = \widehat{w}_1 \widehat{F}_1 + \widehat{w}_2 \widehat{F}_2$ *is* ε-close (on a component-by-component basis) to F if there is a permutation $\pi : \{1, 2\} \to \{1, 2\}$ so that for all $i \in \{1, 2\}$

$$\left| w_i - \widehat{w}_{\pi(i)} \right|, d_{TV}(F_i, \widehat{F}_{\pi(i)}) \leq \varepsilon.$$

Note that F and $\widehat{F}$ must necessarily be close as mixtures too: $d_{TV}(F, \widehat{F}) \leq 4\varepsilon$. However, we can have mixtures F and $\widehat{F}$ that are both mixtures of k Gaussians and are close as distributions, but are not close on a component-by-component basis. So why should we aim for such a challenging goal? It turns out that if $\widehat{F}$ is ε-close to F, then given a typical sample, we can estimate the posterior accurately [94]. What this means is that even if you can't cluster all of your samples into which component they came from, you can still figure out which ones it's possible to be confident about. This is one of the main advantages of parameter learning over some of the weaker learning goals.

It's good to achieve the strongest types of learning goals you can hope for, but you should also remember that lower bounds for these strong learning goals (e.g., parameter learning) do not imply lower bounds for weaker problems (e.g., proper density estimation). We will give algorithms for learning the parameters of a mixture of k Gaussians that run in polynomial time for any $k = O(1)$ but have an exponential dependence on k. But this is necessary, in that there are pairs of mixtures of k Gaussians F and $\widehat{F}$ that are not close on a component-by-component basis but have $d_{TV}(F, \widehat{F}) \leq 2^{-k}$ [114]. So any algorithm for parameter learning would be able to tell them apart, but that takes at least 2^k samples, again by a coupling argument. But maybe for proper density estimation it's possible to get an algorithm that is polynomial in all of the parameters.

Open Question 1 *Is there a* $\mathrm{poly}(n, k, 1/\varepsilon)$ *time algorithm for proper density estimation for mixtures of k Gaussians in n dimensions? What about in one dimension?*

7.4 Clustering-Free Algorithms

Our goal is to learn $\widehat{F}$ that is ε-close to F. Let's first generalize the definition to mixtures of k Gaussians:

Definition 7.4.1 *We will say that a mixture* $\widehat{F} = \sum_{i=1}^{k} \widehat{w}_i \widehat{F}_i$ *is ε-close (on a component-by-component basis) to F if there is a permutation* π : $\{1, 2, \ldots, k\} \to \{1, 2, \ldots, k\}$ *so that for all* $i \in \{1, 2, \ldots, k\}$,

$$\left| w_i - \widehat{w}_{\pi(i)} \right|, d_{TV}(F_i, \widehat{F}_{\pi(i)}) \le \varepsilon.$$

When can we hope to learn an ε close estimate in $\mathrm{poly}(n, 1/\varepsilon)$ samples? There are two situations where it just isn't possible. Eventually our algorithm will show that these are the only things that go wrong:

(a) If $w_i = 0$, we can never learn $\widehat{F}_i$ that is close to F_i, because we never get any samples from F_i.

In fact, we need a quantitative lower bound on each w_i, say $w_i \ge \varepsilon$, so that if we take a reasonable number of samples, we will get at least one sample from each component.

(b) If $d_{TV}(F_i, F_j) = 0$, we can never learn w_i or w_j, because F_i and F_j entirely overlap.

Again, we need a quantitative lower bound on $d_{TV}(F_i, F_j)$, say $d_{TV}(F_i, F_j) \ge \varepsilon$, for each $i \ne j$ so that if we take a reasonable number of samples, we will get at least one sample from the nonoverlap region between various pairs of components.

Theorem 7.4.2 *[94], [114] If $w_i \ge \varepsilon$ for each i and $d_{TV}(F_i, F_j) \ge \varepsilon$ for each $i \ne j$, then there is an efficient algorithm that learns an ε-close estimate $\widehat{F}$ to F whose running time and sample complexity are $\mathrm{poly}(n, 1/\varepsilon, \log 1/\delta)$ and that succeeds with probability $1 - \delta$.*

Note that the degree of the polynomial depends polynomially on k. Kalai, Moitra, and Valiant [94] gave the first algorithm for learning mixtures of two Gaussians with no separation conditions. Subsequently, Moitra and Valiant [114] gave an algorithm for mixtures of k Gaussians, again with no separation conditions.

In independent and concurrent work, Belkin and Sinha [28] gave a polynomial time algorithm for mixtures of k Gaussians too; however, there is no explicit bound given on the running time as a function of k (since their work depends on Hilbert's basis theorem, which is fundamentally ineffective). Also, the goal in [94] and [114] is to learn $\widehat{F}$ so that its components are close in total variation distance to those of F, which is in general a stronger goal than requiring that the parameters be additively close, which is the goal in [28]. The benefit is that the algorithm in [28] works for more general learning problems in the one-dimensional setting, and we will explain the ideas of their algorithm at the end of this chapter.

Throughout this section we will focus on the $k = 2$ case, since this algorithm is conceptually much simpler. In fact, we will aim for a weaker learning goal: We will say that $\widehat{F}$ is *additively* ε-*close* to F if $|w_i - \widehat{w}_{\pi(i)}|$, $\|\mu_i - \widehat{\mu}_{\pi(i)}\|$, $\|\Sigma_i - \widehat{\Sigma}_{\pi(i)}\|_F \leq \varepsilon$ for all i. We want to find such an $\widehat{F}$. It turns out that we will be able to assume that F is normalized in the following sense:

Definition 7.4.3 *A distribution F is in isotropic position if*

(a) $\mathbb{E}_{x \leftarrow F}[x] = 0$ *and*
(b) $\mathbb{E}_{x \leftarrow F}[xx^T] = I$.

The second condition means that the variance is one in *every* direction. Actually, it's easy to put a distribution in isotropic position, provided that there's no direction where the variance is zero. More precisely:

Claim 7.4.4 *If* $\mathbb{E}_{x \leftarrow F}[xx^T]$ *is full rank, then there is an affine transformation that places F in isotropic position.*

Proof: Let $\mu = E_{x \leftarrow F}[x]$. Then

$$E_{x \leftarrow F}[(x - \mu)(x - \mu)^T] = M = BB^T$$

which follows because M is positive semidefinite and hence has a Cholesky decomposition. By assumption, M has full rank, and hence B does too. Now if we set

$$y = B^{-1}(x - \mu)$$

it is easy to see that $\mathbb{E}[y] = 0$ and $\mathbb{E}[yy^T] = B^{-1}M(B^{-1})^T = I$ as desired. ∎

Our goal is to learn an additive ε approximation to F, and we will assume that F has been preprocessed so that it is in isotropic position.

Outline

We can now describe the basic outline of the algorithm, although there will be many details to fill in:

(a) Consider a series of projections down to one dimension.
(b) Run a univariate learning algorithm.
(c) Set up a system of linear equations on the high-dimensional parameters and back-solve.

Isotropic Projection Lemma

We will need to overcome a number of obstacles to realize this plan, but let's work through the details of this outline. First let's understand what happens to the parameters of a Gaussian when we project it along some direction r:

Claim 7.4.5 $proj_r[\mathcal{N}(\mu, \Sigma)] = \mathcal{N}(r^T \mu, r^T \Sigma r)$

This simple claim already tells us something important: Suppose we want to learn the parameters μ and Σ of a high-dimensional Gaussian. If we project it onto direction r and learn the parameters of the resulting one-dimensional Gaussian, then what we've really learned are linear constraints on μ and Σ. If we do this many times for many different directions r, we could hope to get enough linear constraints on μ and Σ that we could simply solve for them. Moreover, it's natural to hope that we need only about n^2 directions, because there are that many parameters of Σ. But now we're coming up to the first problem we'll need to find a way around. Let's introduce some notation:

Definition 7.4.6 $d_p(\mathcal{N}(\mu_1, \sigma_1^2), \mathcal{N}(\mu_2, \sigma_2^2)) = |\mu_1 - \mu_2| + |\sigma_1^2 - \sigma_2^2|$

We will refer to this as the parameter distance. Ultimately, we will give a univariate algorithm for learning mixtures of Gaussians, and we would like to run it on $proj_r[F]$.

Problem 2 *But what if $d_p(proj_r[F_1], proj_r[F_2])$ is exponentially small?*

This would be a problem, since we would need to run our univariate algorithm with exponentially fine precision just to see that there are two components and not one! How can we get around this issue? We'll prove that this problem essentially never arises when F is in isotropic position. For intuition, consider two cases:

(a) Suppose $\|\mu_1 - \mu_2\| \geq \text{poly}(1/n, \varepsilon)$.

You can think of this condition as just saying that $\|\mu_1 - \mu_2\|$ is not exponentially small. In any case, we know that projecting a vector onto a random direction typically reduces its norm by a factor of $\sqrt{n}$ and that its projected length is concentrated around this value. This tells us that with high probability $\|r^T \mu_1 - r^T \mu_2\|$ is at least $\text{poly}(1/n, \varepsilon)$ too. Hence $\text{proj}_r[F_1]$ and $\text{proj}_r[F_2]$ will have noticeably different parameters just due to the difference in their means.

(b) Otherwise, $\|\mu_1 - \mu_2\| \leq \text{poly}(1/n, \varepsilon)$.

The key idea is that if $d_{TV}(F_1, F_2) \geq \varepsilon$ and their means are exponentially close, then their covariances Σ_1 and Σ_2 must be noticeably different when projected on a random direction r. In this case, $\text{proj}_r[F_1]$ and $\text{proj}_r[F_2]$ will have noticeably different parameters due to the difference in their variances. This is the intuition behind the following lemma:

Lemma 7.4.7 *If F is in isotropic position and $w_i \geq \varepsilon$ and $d_{TV}(F_1, F_2) \geq \varepsilon$, then with high probability for a direction r chosen uniformly at random*

$$d_p(\text{proj}_r[F_1], \text{proj}_r[F_2]) \geq \varepsilon_3 = \text{poly}(1/n, \varepsilon).$$

This lemma is false when F is not in isotropic position (e.g., consider the parallel pancakes example)! It also fails when generalizing to mixtures of $k > 2$ Gaussians even when the mixture is in isotropic position. What goes wrong is that there are examples where projecting onto almost all directions r essentially results in a mixture with strictly fewer components! (The approach in [114] is to learn a mixture of fewer Gaussians as a proxy for the true mixture, and later on find a direction that can be used to separate out pairs of components that have been merged.)

Pairing Lemma

Next we will encounter the second problem: Suppose we project onto direction r and s and learn $\widehat{F^r} = \frac{1}{2}\widehat{F_1^r} + \frac{1}{2}\widehat{F_2^r}$ and $\widehat{F^s} = \frac{1}{2}\widehat{F_1^s} + \frac{1}{2}\widehat{F_2^s}$, respectively. Then the mean and variance of $\widehat{F_1^r}$ yield a linear constraint on one of the two high-dimensional Gaussians, and similarly for $\widehat{F_1^s}$.

Problem 3 *How do we know that they yield constraints on the same high-dimensional component?*

Ultimately we want to set up a system of linear constraints to solve for the parameters of F_1, but when we project F onto different directions (say,

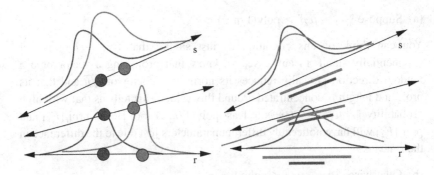

Figure 7.2: The projected mean and projected variance vary continuously as we sweep from r to s.

r and s), we need to pair up the components from these two directions. The key observation is that as we vary r to s, the parameters of the mixture vary continuously. (See Figure 7.2). Hence when we project onto r, we know from the isotropic projection lemma that the two components will have either noticeably different means or variances. Suppose their means are different by ε_3; then if r and s are close (compared to ε_1), the parameters of each component in the mixture do not change much and the component in $\text{proj}_r[F]$ with larger mean will correspond to the same component as the one in $\text{proj}_s[F]$ with larger mean. A similar statement applies when it is the variances that are at least ε_3 apart.

Lemma 7.4.8 *If $\|r - s\| \leq \varepsilon_2 = \text{poly}(1/n, \varepsilon_3)$, then:*

(a) *If $|r^T \mu_1 - r^T \mu_2| \geq \varepsilon_3$, then the components in $\text{proj}_r[F]$ and $\text{proj}_s[F]$ with the larger mean correspond to the same high-dimensional component.*

(b) *Else if $|r^T \Sigma_1 r - r^T \Sigma_2 r| \geq \varepsilon_3$, then the components in $\text{proj}_r[F]$ and $\text{proj}_s[F]$ with the larger variance correspond to the same high-dimensional component.*

Hence if we choose r randomly and only search over directions s with $\|r - s\| \leq \varepsilon_2$, we will be able to pair up the components correctly in the different one-dimensional mixtures.

Condition Number Lemma

Now we encounter the final problem in the high-dimensional case: Suppose we choose r randomly, and for $s_1, s_2, \ldots, s_p$ we learn the parameters of the projection of F onto these directions and pair up the components correctly. We can only hope to learn the parameters on these projections up to some additive accuracy ε_1 (and our univariate learning algorithm will have running time and sample complexity $\text{poly}(1/\varepsilon_1)$).

Problem 4 *How do these errors in our univariate estimates translate to errors in our high-dimensional estimates for* $\mu_1, \Sigma_1, \mu_2, \Sigma_2$?

Recall that the *condition number* controls this. The final lemma we need in the high-dimensional case is:

Lemma 7.4.9 *The condition number of the linear system to solve for* μ_1, Σ_1 *is* $\text{poly}(1/\varepsilon_2, n)$ *where all pairs of directions are* ε_2 *apart.*

Intuitively, as r and $s_1, s_2, \ldots, s_p$ are closer together, the condition number of the system will be worse (because the linear constraints are closer to redundant), but the key fact is that the condition number is bounded by a fixed polynomial in $1/\varepsilon_2$ and n, and hence if we choose $\varepsilon_1 = \text{poly}(\varepsilon_2, n)\varepsilon$, then our estimates of the high-dimensional parameters will be within an additive ε. Note that each parameter $\varepsilon, \varepsilon_3, \varepsilon_2, \varepsilon_1$ is a fixed polynomial in the earlier parameters (and $1/n$), and hence we need only run our univariate learning algorithm with inverse polynomial precision on a polynomial number of mixtures to learn an ε-close estimate $\widehat{F}$!

But we still need to design a univariate algorithm, and next we return to Pearson's original problem!

7.5 A Univariate Algorithm

Here we will give a univariate algorithm for learning the parameters of a mixture of two Gaussians up to additive accuracy ε whose running time and sample complexity is $\text{poly}(1/\varepsilon)$. Our first observation is that all of the parameters are bounded:

Claim 7.5.1 *Let* $F = w_1 F_1 + w_2 F_2$ *be a mixture of two Gaussians that is in isotropic position. Suppose that* $w_1, w_2 \geq \varepsilon$. *Then*

(a) $\mu_1, \mu_2 \in [-1/\sqrt{\varepsilon}, 1/\sqrt{\varepsilon}]$ *and*
(b) $\sigma_1^2, \sigma_2^2 \in [0, 1/\varepsilon]$.

The idea is that if either of the conditions is violated, it would imply that the mixture has variance strictly larger than one. Once we know that the parameters are bounded, the natural approach is to try a grid search:

Grid Search

Input: Samples from $F(\Theta)$
Output: Parameters $\widehat{\Theta} = (\widehat{w}_1, \widehat{\mu}_1, \widehat{\sigma}_1^2, \widehat{\mu}_2, \widehat{\sigma}_2^2)$

For all valid $\widehat{\Theta}$ where the parameters are multiples of ε^C
    Test $\widehat{\Theta}$ using the samples, if it passes output $\widehat{\Theta}$
End

There are many ways we could think about testing the closeness of our estimate with the true parameters of the model. For example, we could empirically estiamte the first six moments of $F(\Theta)$ from our samples, and pass $\widehat{\Theta}$ if its first six moments are each within some additive tolerance τ of the empirical moments. (This is really a variant on Pearson's sixth moment test.) It is easy to see that if we take enough samples and set τ appropriately, then if we round the true parameters Θ to any valid grid point whose parameters are multiples of ε^C, the resulting $\widehat{\Theta}$ will with high probability pass our test. This is called the *completeness*. The much more challenging part is establishing the *soundness*; after all, why is there no other set of parameters $\widehat{\Theta}$ except for ones close to Θ that pass our test?

Alternatively, we want to prove that any two mixtures F and $\widehat{F}$ whose parameters *do not* match within an additive ε must have one of their first six moments noticeably different. The main lemma is:

Lemma 7.5.2 (Six Moments Suffice) *For any F and $\widehat{F}$ that are not ε-close in parameters, there is an $r \in \{1, 2, \ldots, 6\}$ where*

$$\left| M_r(\Theta) - M_r(\widehat{\Theta}) \right| \geq \varepsilon^{O(1)}$$

where Θ and $\widehat{\Theta}$ are the parameters of F and $\widehat{F}$, respectively, and M_r is the rth raw moment.

Let $\widetilde{M}_r$ be the empirical moments. Then

$$\left| M_r(\widehat{\Theta}) - M_r(\Theta) \right| \leq \underbrace{\left| \widetilde{M}_r(\widehat{\Theta}) - \widetilde{M}_r \right|}_{\leq \tau} + \underbrace{\left| \widetilde{M}_r - M_r(\Theta) \right|}_{\leq \tau} \leq 2\tau$$

where the first term is at most τ because the test passes, and the second term is small because we can take enough samples (but still poly$(1/\tau)$) so that the empirical moments and the true moments are close. Hence we can apply the above lemma in the contrapositive, and conclude that if the grid search outputs

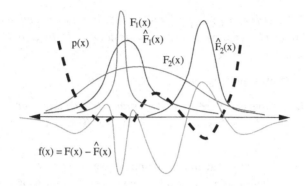

Figure 7.3: If $f(x)$ has at most six zero crossings, we can find a polynomial of degree at most six that agrees with its sign.

$\widehat{\Theta}$, then Θ and $\widehat{\Theta}$ must be ε-close in parameters, which gives us an efficient univariate algorithm!

So our main goal is to prove that if F and $\widehat{F}$ are not ε-close, one of their first six moments is noticeably different. In fact, even the case of $\varepsilon = 0$ is challenging: If F and $\widehat{F}$ are different mixtures of two Gaussians, why is one of their first six moments necessarily different? Our main goal is to prove this statement using the *heat equation*.

In fact, let us consider the following thought experiment. Let $f(x) = F(x) - \widehat{F}(x)$ be the pointwise difference between the density functions F and $\widehat{F}$. Then the heart of the problem is: Can we prove that $f(x)$ crosses the x-axis at most six times? (See Figure 7.3.)

Lemma 7.5.3 *If $f(x)$ crosses the x-axis at most six times, then one of the first six moments of F and $\widehat{F}$ is different.*

Proof: In fact, we can construct a (nonzero) degree at most six polynomial $p(x)$ that agrees with the sign of $f(x)$; i.e., $p(x)f(x) \geq 0$ for all x. Then

$$0 < \left| \int_x p(x)f(x)dx \right| = \left| \int_x \sum_{r=1}^6 p_r x^r f(x)dx \right|$$

$$\leq \sum_{r=1}^6 |p_r| \left| M_r(\Theta) - M_r(\widehat{\Theta}) \right|.$$

And if the first six moments of F and $\widehat{F}$ match exactly, the right-hand side is zero, which is a contradiction. ∎

So all we need to prove is that $F(x) - \widehat{F}(x)$ has at most six zero crossings. Let us prove a stronger lemma by induction:

Lemma 7.5.4 *Let $f(x) = \sum_{i=1}^{k} \alpha_i \mathcal{N}(\mu_i, \sigma_i^2, x)$ be a linear combination of k Gaussians (α_i can be negative). Then if $f(x)$ is not identically zero, $f(x)$ has at most $2k - 2$ zero crossings.*

We will rely on the following tools:

Theorem 7.5.5 *Given $f(x) : \mathbb{R} \to \mathbb{R}$ that is analytic and has n zero crossings, then for any $\sigma^2 > 0$, the function $g(x) = f(x) * \mathcal{N}(0, \sigma^2)$ has at most n zero crossings.*

This theorem has a physical interpretation. If we think of $f(x)$ as the heat profile of an infinite one-dimensional rod, then what does the heat profile look like at some later time? In fact, it is precisely $g(x) = f(x) * \mathcal{N}(0, \sigma^2)$ for an appropriately chosen σ^2. Alternatively, the Gaussian is the *Green's function* of the heat equation. And hence many of our physical intuitions for diffusion have consequences for convolution – convolving a function by a Gaussian has the effect of smoothing it, and it cannot create new local maxima (and relatedly, it cannot create new zero crossings).

Finally, we recall the elementary fact:

Fact 7.5.6 $\mathcal{N}(0, \sigma_1^2) * \mathcal{N}(0, \sigma_2^2) = \mathcal{N}(0, \sigma_1^2 + \sigma_2^2)$

Now, we are ready to prove the above lemma and conclude that if we knew the first six moments of a mixture of two Gaussians, *exactly*, then we would know its parameters exactly too. Let us prove the above lemma by induction, and assume that for any linear combination of $k = 3$ Gaussians, the number of zero crossings is at most four. Now consider an arbitrary linear combination of four Gaussians, and let σ^2 be the smallest variance of any component. (See Figure 7.4a.) We can consider a related mixture where we subtract σ^2 from the variance of each component. (See Figure 7.4b.)

Now, if we ignore the delta function, we have a linear combination of three Gaussians, and by induction we know that it has at most four zero crossings. But how many zero crossings can we add when we add back in the delta function? We can add at most two, one on the way up and one on the way down (here we are ignoring some real analysis complications of working with delta functions for ease of presentation). (See Figure 7.4c.) And now we can convolve the function by $\mathcal{N}(0, \sigma^2)$ to recover the original linear combination of four Gaussians, but this last step does not increase the number of zero crossings! (See Figure 7.4d.)

This proves that

$$\left\{ M_r(\widehat{\Theta}) = M_r(\Theta) \right\}, \quad r = 1, 2, \ldots, 6$$

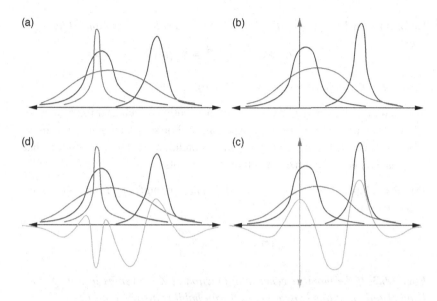

Figure 7.4: (a) Linear combination of four Gaussians; (b) subtracting σ^2 from each variance; (c) adding back in the delta function; (d) convolving by $\mathcal{N}(0, \sigma^2)$ to recover the original linear combination.

has only two solutions (the true parameters, and we can also interchange which is component is which). In fact, this system of polynomial equations is also *stable*, and there is an analogue of condition numbers for systems of polynomial equations that implies a quantitative version of what we have just proved: if F and $\widehat{F}$ are not ε-close, then one of their first six moments is noticeably different. This gives us our univariate algorithm.

7.6 A View from Algebraic Geometry

Here we will present an alternative univariate learning algorithm of Belkin and Sinha [28] that also makes use of the method of moments, but gives a much more general analysis using tools from algebraic geometry.

Polynomial Families

We will analyze the method of moments for the following class of distributions:

Definition 7.6.1 *A class of distributions* $F(\Theta)$ *is called a polynomial family if*

$$\forall r, \ \mathbb{E}_{X \in F(\Theta)} \left[X^r \right] = M_r(\Theta)$$

where $M_r(\Theta)$ *is a polynomial in* $\Theta = (\theta_1, \theta_2, \ldots, \theta_k)$.

This definition captures a broad class of distributions, such as mixture models whose components are uniform, exponential, Poisson, Gaussian, or gamma functions. We will need another (tame) condition on the distribution that guarantees it is characterized by all of its moments.

Definition 7.6.2 *The moment-generating function (mgf) of a random variable* X *is defined as*

$$f(t) = \sum_{n=0}^{\infty} \mathbb{E} \left[X^n \right] \frac{t^n}{n!}.$$

Fact 7.6.3 *If the moment-generating function of* X *converges in a neighborhood of zero, it uniquely determines the probability distribution; i.e.,*

$$\forall r, \ M_r(\Theta) = M_r(\widehat{\Theta}) \implies F(\Theta) = F(\widehat{\Theta}).$$

Our goal is to show that for any polynomial family, a *finite* number of its moments suffice. First we introduce the relevant definitions:

Definition 7.6.4 *Given a ring* R, *an ideal* I *generated by* $g_1, g_2, \cdots, g_n \in R$ *denoted by* $I = \langle g_1, g_2, \cdots, g_n \rangle$ *is defined as*

$$I = \left\{ \sum_i r_i g_i \text{ where } r_i \in R \right\}.$$

Definition 7.6.5 *A Noetherian ring is a ring such that for any sequence of ideals*

$$I_1 \subseteq I_2 \subseteq I_3 \subseteq \cdots,$$

there is N *such that* $I_N = I_{N+1} = I_{N+2} = \cdots$.

Theorem 7.6.6 *[Hilbert's Basis Theorem] If* R *is a Noetherian ring, then* $R[X]$ *is also a Noetherian ring.*

It is easy to see that $\mathbb{R}$ is a Noetherian ring, and hence we know that $\mathbb{R}[x]$ is also Noetherian. Now we can prove that for any polynomial family, a finite number of moments suffice to uniquely identify any distribution in the family:

Theorem 7.6.7 *Let $F(\Theta)$ be a polynomial family. If the moment-generating function converges in a neighborhood of zero, there exists N such that*

$$F(\Theta) = F(\widehat{\Theta}) \text{ if and only if } M_r(\Theta) = M_r(\widehat{\Theta}) \ \forall r \in 1, 2, \cdots, N.$$

Proof: Let $Q_r(\Theta, \widehat{\Theta}) = M_r(\Theta) - M_r(\widehat{\Theta})$. Let $I_1 = \langle Q_1 \rangle$, $I_2 = \langle Q_1, Q_2 \rangle$, $\cdots$. This is our ascending chain of ideals in $\mathbb{R}[\Theta, \widehat{\Theta}]$. We can invoke Hilbert's basis theorem and conclude that $\mathbb{R}[X]$ is a Noetherian ring, and hence there is N such that $I_N = I_{N+1} = \cdots$. So for all $N + j$, we have

$$Q_{N+j}(\Theta, \widehat{\Theta}) = \sum_{i=1}^{N} p_{ij}(\Theta, \widehat{\Theta}) Q_i(\Theta, \widehat{\Theta})$$

for some polynomial $p_{ij} \in \mathbb{R}[\Theta, \widehat{\Theta}]$. Thus, if $M_r(\Theta) = M_r(\widehat{\Theta})$ for all $r \in 1, 2, \cdots, N$, then $M_r(\Theta) = M_r(\widehat{\Theta})$ for all r, and from Fact 7.6.3 we conclude that $F(\Theta) = F(\widehat{\Theta})$.

The other side of the theorem is obvious. ∎

The theorem above does not give any finite bound on N, since the basis theorem does not either. This is because the basis theorem is proved by contradiction, but more fundamentally, it is not possible to give a bound on N that depends only on the choice of the ring. Consider the following example:

Example 2 *Consider the Noetherian ring $\mathbb{R}[x]$. Let $I_i = \langle x^{N-i} \rangle$ for $i = 0, \cdots, N$. It is a strictly ascending chain of ideals for $i = 0, \cdots, N$. Therefore, even if the ring $\mathbb{R}[x]$ is fixed, there is no universal bound on N.*

Bounds such as those in Theorem 7.6.7 are often referred to as *ineffective*. Consider an application of the above result to mixtures of Gaussians: from the above theorem, we have that any two mixtures F and $\widehat{F}$ of k Gaussians are identical if and only if these mixtures agree on their first N moments. Here N is a function of k and N is finite, but we cannot write down any explicit bound on N as a function of k using the above tools. Nevertheless, these tools apply much more broadly than the specialized ones based on the heat equation that we used in the previous section to prove that $4k - 2$ moments suffice for mixtures of k Gaussians.

Systems of Polynomial Inequalities

In general, we do not have exact access to the moments of a distribution, but only noisy approximations. Our main goal is to prove a quantitative version of the previous result that shows that any two distributions F and $\widehat{F}$ that are close on their first N moments are close in their parameters too. The key fact is that we can bound the condition number of systems of polynomial inequalities; there are a number of ways to do this, but we will use *quantifier elimination.* Recall:

Definition 7.6.8 *A set S is semialgebraic if there exist multivariate polynomials $p_1, \ldots, p_n$ such that*

$$S = \{x_1, \ldots, x_r | p_i(x_1, \ldots, x_r) \geq 0\}$$

or if S is a finite union or intersection of such sets.

When a set can be defined through polynomial equalities, we call it *algebraic.*

Theorem 7.6.9 *[Tarski] The projection of a semialgebraic set is semialgebraic.*

Interestingly, the projection of an algebraic set is not necessarily algebraic. Can you come up with an example? A projection corresponds to defining a set not just through polynomial inequalities, but also a $\exists$ operator. It turns out that you can even take a sequence of $\exists$ and $\forall$ operators and the resulting set is still semialgebraic.

With this tool in hand, we define the following helper set:

$$H(\varepsilon, \delta) = \left\{ \forall(\Theta, \widehat{\Theta}) \; : \; |M_r(\Theta) - M_r(\widehat{\Theta})| \leq \delta \text{ for } r = 1, 2, \ldots N \implies d_p(\Theta, \widehat{\Theta}) \leq \varepsilon \right\}$$

Here $d_p(\Theta, \widehat{\Theta})$ is some parameter distance between Θ and $\widehat{\Theta}$. It is not important exactly what we choose, just that it can be expressed through polynomials in the parameters and that it treats parameters that produce the same distribution as the same; e.g., by taking the minimum over all matchings of components in $F(\Theta)$ to components in $F(\widehat{\Theta})$ and summing the componentwise parameter distances.

Now let $\varepsilon(\delta)$ be the smallest ε as a function of δ. Using Tarski's theorem, we can prove the following stability bound for the method of moments:

Theorem 7.6.10 *There are fixed constants C_1, C_2, s such that if $\delta \leq 1/C_1$, then $\varepsilon(\delta) \leq C_2 \delta^{1/s}$.*

Proof: It is easy to see that we can define $H(\varepsilon, \delta)$ as the projection of a semialgebraic set, hence using Tarski's theorem, we conclude that $H(\varepsilon, \delta)$ is also semialgebraic. The crucial observation is that because $H(\varepsilon, \delta)$ is semialgebraic, the smallest we can choose ε to be as a function of δ is itself a polynomial function of δ. There are some caveats here, because we need to prove that for a fixed δ we can choose ε to be strictly greater than zero and, moreover, the polynomial relationship between ε and δ only holds if δ is sufficiently small. However, these technical issues can be resolved without much more work (see [28]). ■

Now we arrive at the main result:

Corollary 7.6.11 *If* $|M_r(\Theta) - M_r(\widehat{\Theta})| \leq \left(\frac{\varepsilon}{C_2}\right)^s$, *then* $d_p(\Theta, \widehat{\Theta}) \leq \varepsilon$.

Hence there is a polynomial time algorithm to learn the parameters of any univariate polynomial family (whose mgf converges in a neighborhood of zero) within an additive accuracy of ε whose running time and sample complexity is poly($1/\varepsilon$); we can take enough samples to estimate the first N moments within ε^s and search over a grid of the parameters, and any set of parameters that matches each of the moments is necessarily close in parameter distance to the true parameters.

7.7 Exercises

Problem 7-1: Suppose we are given a mixture of two Gaussians where the variances of each component are equal:

$$F(x) = w_1 \mathcal{N}(\mu_1, \sigma^2, x) + (1 - w_1)\mathcal{N}(\mu_2, \sigma^2, x)$$

Show that four moments suffice to uniquely determine the parameters of the mixture.

Problem 7-2: Suppose we are given access to an oracle that, for any direction r, returns the projected means and variances; i.e., $r^T \mu_1$ and $r^T \Sigma_1 r$ for one component and $r^T \mu_2$ and $r^T \Sigma_2 r$. The trouble is that you do not know which parameters correspond to which component.

(a) Design an algorithm to recover μ_1 and μ_2 (up to permuting which component is which) that makes at most $O(d^2)$ queries to the oracle where d is the dimension. *Hint:* Recover the entries of $(\mu_1 - \mu_2)(\mu_1 - \mu_2)^T$.

(b) **Challenge:** Design an algorithm to recover Σ_1 and Σ_2 (up to permuting which component is which) that makes $O(1)$ queries to the oracle when $d = 2$.

Note that here we are not assuming anything about how far apart the projected means or variances are on some direction r.

8
Matrix Completion

In earlier chapters, we saw the power of sparsity. It's possible to recover a sparse vector from many fewer measurements than its dimension. And if we don't know the basis where our vectors are sparse, with enough examples we can learn it. But sparsity is just the beginning. There are many other ways to make the objects we are working with be low-complexity. In this chapter, we will study the matrix completion problem, where the goal is to reconstruct a matrix even when we observe just a few of its entries. Without any assumptions on the matrix, this is impossible, because there are just too many degrees of freedom. But when the matrix is low-rank and incoherent, it turns out that there are simple convex programs that work. You can take these ideas much further and study all sorts of structured recovery problems via convex programs, such as decomposing a matrix into the sum of a sparse matrix and a low-rank matrix. We won't get to these here, but will give pointers to the literature.

8.1 Introduction

In 2006, Netflix issued a grand challenge to the machine learning community: Beat our prediction algorithms for recommending movies to users by more than 10 percent, and we'll give you a million dollars. It took a few years, but eventually the challenge was won and Netflix paid out. During that time, we all learned a lot about how to build good recommendation systems. In this chapter, we will cover one of the main ingredients, which is called the matrix completion problem.

The starting point is to model our problem of predicting movie ratings as a problem of predicting the unobserved entries of a matrix from the ones we do observe. More precisely, if user i rates movie j (from one to five stars), we set $M_{i,j}$ to be the numerical score. Our goal is to use the entries $M_{i,j}$ that we observe to predict the ones that we don't know. If we could predict these accurately, it would give us a way to suggest movies to users in a way that we are suggesting movies that we think they might like. A priori, there's no reason to believe you can do this. If we think about the entire matrix M that we would get by coercing every user to rate every movie (and in the Netflix dataset there are $480,189$ users and $17,770$ movies), then in principle the entries $M_{i,j}$ that we observe might tell us nothing about the unobserved entries.

We're in the same conundrum we were in when we talked about compressed sensing. A priori, there is no reason to believe you can take fewer linear measurements of a vector x than its dimension and reconstruct x. What we need is some assumption about the structure. In compressed sensing, we assumed that x is sparse or approximately sparse. In matrix completion, we will assume that M is low-rank or approximately low-rank. It's important to think about where this assumption comes from. If M were low-rank, we could write it as

$$M = u^{(1)}(v^{(1)})^T + u^{(2)}(v^{(2)})^T \dots u^{(r)}(v^{(r)})^T.$$

The hope is that each of these rank-one terms represents some category of movies. For example, the first term might represent the category *drama*, and the entries in $u^{(1)}$ might represent for every user, to what extent does he or she like drama movies? Then each entry in $v^{(1)}$ would represent for every movie, to what extent would it appeal to someone who likes drama? This is where the low-rank assumption comes from. What we're hoping is that there are some categories underlying our data that make it possible to fill in missing entries. When I have a user's ratings for movies in each of the categories, I could then recommend other movies in the category that he or she likes by leveraging the data I have from other users.

The Model and Main Results

Now let's be formal. Suppose there are n users and m movies so that M is an $n \times m$ matrix. Let $\Omega \subseteq [n] \times [m]$ be the indices where we observe the value $M_{i,j}$. Our goal is, under the assumption that M is low-rank or approximately low-rank, to fill in the missing entries. The trouble is that in this level of generality, finding the matrix M of lowest rank that agrees with our observations is *NP*-hard. However, there are some by now standard assumptions under which we will be able to give efficient algorithms for recovering M exactly:

(a) The entries we observe are chosen uniformly at random from $[n] \times [m]$.
(b) M has rank r.
(c) The singular vectors of M are uncorrelated with the standard basis (such a matrix is called *incoherent* and we define this later).

In this chapter, our main result is that there are efficient algorithms for recovering M exactly if $m \approx mr \log m$ where $m \geq n$ and rank$(M) \leq r$. This is similar to compressed sensing, where we were able to recover a k-sparse signal x from $O(k \log n/k)$ linear measurements, which is much smaller than the dimension of x. Here too we can recover a low-rank matrix M from a number of observations that is much smaller than the dimension of M.

Let us examine the assumptions above. The assumption that should give us pause is that Ω is uniformly random. This is somewhat unnatural, since it would be more believable if the probability that we observe $M_{i,j}$ depended on the value itself. Alternatively, a user should be more likely to rate a movie *if he or she actually liked it*.

We already discussed the second assumption. In order to understand the third assumption, suppose our observations are indeed uniformly random. Consider

$$M = \Pi \left[\begin{array}{c|c} I_r & 0 \\ \hline 0 & 0 \end{array} \right] \Pi^T$$

where Π is a uniformly random permutation matrix. M is low-rank, but unless we observe all of the ones along the diagonal, we will not be able to recover M uniquely. Indeed, the top singular vectors of M are standard basis vectors. But if we were to assume that the singular vectors of M are incoherent with respect to the standard basis, we would avoid this snag, because the vectors in our low-rank decomposition of M are spread out over many rows and columns.

Definition 8.1.1 *The coherence μ of a subspace $U \subseteq \mathbb{R}^n$ of dimension $dim(u) = r$ is*

$$\frac{n}{r} \max_i \|P_U e_i\|^2$$

where P_U denotes the orthogonal projection onto U and e_i is the standard basis element.

It is easy to see that if we choose U uniformly at random, then $\mu(U) = \tilde{O}(1)$. Also we have that $1 \leq \mu(U) \leq n/r$ and the upper bound is attained if U contains any e_i. We can now see that if we set U to be the top singular vectors of the above example, then U has high coherence. We will need the following conditions on M:

(a) Let $M = U\Sigma V^T$, then $\mu(U), \mu(V) \leq \mu_0$.
(b) $\|UV^T\|_\infty \leq \frac{\mu_1 \sqrt{r}}{\sqrt{nm}}$, where $\|\cdot\|_\infty$ denotes the maximum absolute value of any entry.

The main result of this chapter is:

Theorem 8.1.2 *Suppose* Ω *is chosen uniformly at random. Then there is a polynomial time algorithm to recover* M *exactly that succeeds with high probability if*

$$|\Omega| \geq C \max(\mu_1^2, \mu_0) r(n+m) \log^2(n+m).$$

The algorithm in the theorem above is based on a convex relaxation for the rank of a matrix called the *nuclear norm*. We will introduce this in the next section and establish some of its properties, but one can think of it as an analogue to the ℓ_1 minimization approach that we used in compressed sensing. This approach was first introduced in Fazel's thesis [70], and Recht, Fazel, and Parrilo [124] proved that this approach exactly recovers M in the setting of *matrix sensing*, which is related to the problem we consider here.

In a landmark paper, Candes and Recht [41] proved that the relaxation based on nuclear norm also succeeds for matrix completion and introduced the assumptions above in order to prove that their algorithm works. There has since been a long line of work improving the requirements on m, and the theorem above and our exposition will follow a recent paper of Recht [123] that greatly simplifies the analysis by making use of matrix analogues of the Bernstein bound and using these in a procedure now called *quantum golfing* that was first introduced by Gross [80].

Remark 8.1.3 *We will restrict to* $M \in \mathbb{R}^{n \times n}$ *and assume* $\mu_0, \mu_1 = \tilde{O}(1)$ *in our analysis, which will reduce the number of parameters we need to keep track of.*

8.2 Nuclear Norm

Here we introduce the nuclear norm, which will be the basis for our algorithms for matrix completion. We will follow an outline parallel to that of compressed sensing. In particular, a natural starting point is the optimization problem:

$$(P_0) \qquad \min \operatorname{rank}(X) \text{ s.t. } X_{i,j} = M_{i,j} \text{ for all } (i,j) \in \Omega$$

This optimization problem is *NP*-hard. If $\sigma(X)$ is the vector of singular values of X, then we can think of the rank of X equivalently as the sparsity of $\sigma(X)$. Recall, in compressed sensing we faced a similar obstacle: finding the sparsest solution to a system of linear equations is also *NP*-hard. But instead we considered the ℓ_1 relaxation and proved that under various conditions, this optimization problem recovers the sparsest solution. Similarly, it is natural to consider the ℓ_1-norm of $\sigma(X)$, which is called the nuclear norm:

Definition 8.2.1 *The nuclear norm of* X *denoted by* $\|X\|_*$ *is* $\|\sigma(X)\|_1$.

We will instead solve the convex program:

$$(P_1) \qquad \min \|X\|_* \text{ s.t. } X_{i,j} = M_{i,j} \text{ for all } (i,j) \in \Omega$$

and our goal is to prove conditions under which the solution to (P_1) is exactly M. Note that this is a convex program because $\|X\|_*$ is a norm, and there are a variety of efficient algorithms to solve the above program.

In fact, for our purposes, a crucial notion is that of a *dual norm*. We will not need this concept in full generality, so we state it for the specific case of the nuclear norm. This concept gives us a method to lower-bound the nuclear norm of a matrix:

Definition 8.2.2 *Let* $\langle X, B \rangle = \sum_{i,j} X_{i,j} B_{i,j} = trace(X^T B)$ *denote the matrix inner product.*

Lemma 8.2.3 $\|X\|_* = \max_{\|B\| \leq 1} \langle X, B \rangle$

To get a feel for this, consider the special case where we restrict X and B to be diagonal. Moreover, let $X = \text{diag}(x)$ and $B = \text{diag}(b)$. Then $\|X\|_* = \|x\|_1$ and the constraint $\|B\| \leq 1$ (the spectral norm of B is at most one) is equivalent to $\|b\|_\infty \leq 1$. So we can recover a more familiar characterization of vector norms in the special case of diagonal matrices:

$$\|x\|_1 = \max_{\|b\|_\infty \leq 1} b^T x$$

Proof: We will only prove one direction of the above lemma. What B should we use to certify the nuclear norm of X? Let $X = U_X \Sigma_X V_X^T$, then we will choose $B = U_X V_X^T$. Then

$$\langle X, B \rangle = \text{trace}(B^T X) = \text{trace}(V_X U_X^T U_X \Sigma_X V_X^T)$$
$$= \text{trace}(V_X \Sigma_X V_X^T) = \text{trace}(\Sigma_X) = \|X\|_*$$

where we have used the basic fact that $\text{trace}(ABC) = \text{trace}(BCA)$. Hence this proves $\|X\|_* \leq \max_{\|B\| \leq 1} \langle X, B \rangle$, and the other direction is not much more difficult (see, e.g., [88]). ∎

How can we show that the solution to (P_1) is M? Our basic approach will be a proof by contradiction. Suppose not; then the solution is $M + Z$ for some Z that is supported in $\overline{\Omega}$. Our goal will be to construct a matrix B of spectral norm at most one for which

$$\|M + Z\|_* \geq \langle M + Z, B \rangle > \|M\|_*.$$

Hence $M + Z$ would not be the optimal solution to (P_1). This strategy is similar to the one in compressed sensing, where we hypothesized some other solution

w that differs from x by a vector y in the kernel of the sensing matrix A. There, our strategy was to use geometric properties of $\ker(A)$ to prove that w has strictly larger ℓ_1 norm than x. The proof here will be in the same spirit, but considerably more technical and involved.

Let us introduce some basic projection operators that will be crucial in our proof. Recall, $M = U\Sigma V^T$, let $u_1, \ldots, u_r$ be columns of U, and let $v_1, \ldots, v_r$ be columns of V. Choose $u_{r+1}, \ldots, u_n$ so that $u_1, \ldots, u_n$ form an orthonormal basis for all of $\mathbb{R}^n$; i.e., $u_{r+1}, \ldots, u_n$ is an arbitrary orthonormal basis of $U^\perp$. Similarly, choose $v_{r+1}, \ldots, v_n$ so that $v_1, \ldots, v_n$ form an orthonormal basis for all of $\mathbb{R}^n$. We will be interested in the following linear spaces over matrices:

Definition 8.2.4 $T = span\{u_i v_j^T \mid 1 \le i \le r \text{ or } 1 \le j \le r \text{ or both}\}$

Then $T^\perp = span\{u_i v_j^T \text{ s.t. } r+1 \le i, j \le n\}$. We have $\dim(T) = r^2 + 2(n-r)r$ and $\dim(T^\perp) = (n-r)^2$. Moreover, we can define the linear operators that project into T and $T^\perp$, respectively:

$$P_{T^\perp}[Z] = \sum_{i=r+1}^{n} \sum_{j=r+1}^{n} \langle Z, u_i v_j^T \rangle \cdot u_i v_j^T = P_{U^\perp} Z P_{V^\perp}.$$

And similarly,

$$P_T[Z] = \sum_{(i,j) \in [n] \times [n] - [r+1,n] \times [r+1,n]} \langle Z, u_i v_j^T \rangle \cdot u_i v_j^T = P_U Z + Z P_V - P_U Z P_V.$$

We are now ready to describe the outline of the proof of Theorem 8.1.2. The proof will be based on the following:

(a) We will assume that a certain helper matrix Y exists, and show that this is enough to imply $\|M + Z\|_* > \|M\|_*$ for any Z supported in Ω.
(b) We will construct such a Y using quantum golfing [80].

Conditions for Exact Recovery

Here we will state the conditions we need on the helper matrix Y and prove that if such a Y exists, then M is the solution to (P_1). We require that Y is supported in Ω and

(a) $\|P_T(Y) - UV^T\|_F \le \sqrt{r/8n}$
(b) $\|P_{T^\perp}(Y)\| \le 1/2$.

We want to prove that for any Z supported in $\overline{\Omega}$, $\|M + Z\|_* > \|M\|_*$. Recall, we want to find a matrix B of spectral norm at most one so that $\langle M + Z, B \rangle > \|M\|_*$. Let $U_\perp$ and $V_\perp$ be singular vectors of $P_{T^\perp}[Z]$. Then consider

$$B = \begin{bmatrix} U & U_\perp \end{bmatrix} \cdot \begin{bmatrix} V^T \\ V_\perp^T \end{bmatrix} = UV^T + U_\perp V_\perp^T.$$

Claim 8.2.5 $\|B\| \leq 1$

Proof: By construction, $U^T U_\perp = 0$ and $V^T V_\perp = 0$, and hence the above expression for B is its singular value decomposition, and the claim now follows. ∎

Hence we can plug in our choice for B and simplify:

$$\begin{aligned}
\|M + Z\|_* &\geq \langle M + Z, B \rangle \\
&= \langle M + Z, UV^T + U_\perp V_\perp^T \rangle \\
&= \underbrace{\langle M, UV^T \rangle}_{\|M\|_*} + \langle Z, UV^T + U_\perp V_\perp^T \rangle
\end{aligned}$$

where in the last line we use the fact that M is orthogonal to $U_\perp V_\perp^T$. Now, using the fact that Y and Z have disjoint supports, we can conclude:

$$\|M + Z\|_* \geq \|M\|_* + \langle Z, UV^T + U_\perp V_\perp^T - Y \rangle$$

Therefore, in order to prove the main result in this section, it suffices to prove that $\langle Z, UV^T + U_\perp V_\perp^T - Y \rangle > 0$. We can expand this quantity in terms of its projection onto T and $T^\perp$ and simplify as follows:

$$\begin{aligned}
\|M + Z\|_* - \|M\|_* &\geq \langle P_T(Z), P_T(UV^T + U_\perp V_\perp^T - Y) \rangle \\
&\quad + \langle P_{T^\perp}(Z), P_{T^\perp}(UV^T + U_\perp V_\perp^T - Y) \rangle \\
&\geq \langle P_T(Z), UV^T - P_T(Y) \rangle + \langle P_{T^\perp}(Z), U_\perp V_\perp^T - P_{T^\perp}(Y) \rangle \\
&\geq \langle P_T(Z), UV^T - P_T(Y) \rangle + \|P_{T^\perp}(Z)\|_* - \langle P_{T^\perp}(Z), P_{T^\perp}(Y) \rangle
\end{aligned}$$

where in the last line we used the fact that $U_\perp$ and $V_\perp$ are the singular vectors of $P_{T^\perp}[Z]$, and hence $\langle U_\perp V_\perp^T, P_{T^\perp}[Z] \rangle = \|P_{T^\perp}[Z]\|_*$.

Now we can invoke the properties of Y that we have assumed in this section, to prove a lower bound on the right-hand side. By property (a) of Y, we have that $\|P_T(Y) - UV^T\|_F \leq \sqrt{\frac{r}{2n}}$. Therefore, we know that the first term $\langle P_T(Z), UV^T - P_T(Y) \rangle \geq -\sqrt{\frac{r}{8n}} \|P_T(Z)\|_F$. By property (b) of Y, we know the operator norm of $P_T^\perp(Y)$ is at most $1/2$. Therefore, the third term $\langle P_{T^\perp}(Z), P_{T^\perp}(Y) \rangle$ is at most $\frac{1}{2}\|P_{T^\perp}(Z)\|_*$. Hence

$$\|M + Z\|_* - \|M\|_* \geq -\sqrt{\frac{r}{8n}} \|P_T(Z)\|_F + \frac{1}{2}\|P_{T^\perp}(Z)\|_* \overset{?}{>} 0.$$

We will show that with high probability over the choice of Ω, the inequality does indeed hold. We defer the proof of this last fact, since it and the construction of the helper matrix Y will both make use of the matrix Bernstein inequality, which we present in the next section.

8.3 Quantum Golfing

What remains is to construct a helper matrix Y and prove that with high probability over Ω, for any matrix Z supported in $\overline{\Omega}$, $\|P_{T^{\perp}}(Z)\|_* > \sqrt{\frac{r}{2n}}\|P_T(Z)\|_F$, to complete the proof we started in the previous section. We will make use of an approach introduced by Gross [80] and follow the proof of Recht in [123], where the strategy is to construct Y iteratively. In each phase, we will invoke concentration results for matrix-valued random variables to prove that the error part of Y decreases geometrically and we make rapid progress in constructing a good helper matrix.

First we will introduce the key concentration result that we will apply in several settings. The following matrix-valued Bernstein inequality first appeared in the work of Ahlswede and Winter related to quantum information theory [6]:

Theorem 8.3.1 *[Noncommutative Bernstein Inequality] Let $X_1 \ldots X_l$ be independent mean 0 matrices of size $d \times d$. Let $\rho_k^2 = \max\{\|\mathbb{E}[X_k X_k^T]\|, \|\mathbb{E}[X_k^T X_k]\|\}$ and suppose $\|X_k\| \le M$ almost surely. Then for $\tau > 0$,*

$$\Pr\left[\left\|\sum_{k=1}^{l} X_k\right\| > \tau\right] \le 2d \exp\left\{\frac{-\tau^2/2}{\sum_k \rho_k^2 + M\tau/3}\right\}.$$

If $d = 1$, this is the standard Bernstein inequality. If $d > 1$ and the matrices X_k are diagonal, then this inequality can be obtained from the union bound and the standard Bernstein inequality again. However, to build intuition, consider the following toy problem. Let u_k be a random unit vector in $\mathbb{R}^d$ and let $X_k = u_k u_k^T$. Then it is easy to see that $\rho_k^2 = 1/d$. How many trials do we need so that $\sum_k X_k$ is close to the identity (after scaling)? We should expect to need $\Theta(d \log d)$ trials; this is true even if u_k is drawn uniformly at random from the standard basis vectors $\{e_1 \ldots e_d\}$ due to the coupon collector problem. Indeed, the above bound corroborates our intuition that $\Theta(d \log d)$ is necessary and sufficient.

Now we will apply the above inequality to build up the tools we will need to finish the proof.

Definition 8.3.2 *Let R_{Ω} be the operator that zeros out all the entries of a matrix except those in Ω.*

Lemma 8.3.3 *If Ω is chosen uniformly at random and $m \geq nr \log n$, then with high probability*

$$\frac{n^2}{m} \left\| P_T R_\Omega P_T - \frac{m}{n^2} P_T \right\| < \frac{1}{2}.$$

Remark 8.3.4 *Here we are interested in bounding the operator norm of a linear operator on matrices. Let T be such an operator, then $\|T\|$ is defined as*

$$\max_{\|Z\|_F \leq 1} \|T(Z)\|_F.$$

We will explain how this bound fits into the framework of the matrix Bernstein inequality, but for a full proof, see [123]. Note that $\mathbb{E}[P_T R_\Omega P_T] = P_T \mathbb{E}[R_\Omega] P_T = \frac{m}{n^2} P_T$, and so we just need to show that $P_T R_\Omega P_T$ does not deviate too far from its expectation. Let $e_1, e_2, \ldots, e_d$ be the standard basis vectors. Then we can expand:

$$P_T(Z) = \sum_{a,b} \left\langle P_T(Z), e_a e_b^T \right\rangle e_a e_b^T$$

$$= \sum_{a,b} \left\langle Z, P_T(e_a e_b^T) \right\rangle e_a e_b^T$$

Hence $R_\Omega P_T(Z) = \sum_{(a,b) \in \Omega} \left\langle Z, P_T(e_a e_b^T) \right\rangle e_a e_b^T$, and finally we conclude that

$$P_T R_\Omega P_T(Z) = \sum_{(a,b) \in \Omega} \left\langle Z, P_T(e_a e_b^T) \right\rangle P_T(e_a e_b^T).$$

We can think of $P_T R_\Omega P_T$ as the sum of random operators of the form $\tau_{a,b}$: $Z \to \left\langle Z, P_T(e_a e_b^T) \right\rangle P_T(e_a e_b^T)$, and the lemma follows by applying the matrix Bernstein inequality to the random operator $\sum_{(a,b) \in \Omega} \tau_{a,b}$.

We can now complete the deferred proof of part (a):

Lemma 8.3.5 *If Ω is chosen uniformly at random and $m \geq nr \log n$, then with high probability for any Z supported in $\overline{\Omega}$ we have*

$$\|P_{T^\perp}(Z)\|_* > \sqrt{\frac{r}{2n}} \|P_T(Z)\|_F.$$

Proof: Using Lemma 8.3.3 and the definition of the operator norm (see the remark), we have

$$\left\langle Z, P_T R_\Omega P_T Z - \frac{m}{n^2} P_T Z \right\rangle \geq -\frac{m}{2n^2} \|Z\|_F^2.$$

Furthermore, we can upper-bound the left-hand side as

$$\langle Z, P_T R_\Omega P_T Z \rangle = \langle Z, P_T R_\Omega^2 P_T Z \rangle = \|R_\Omega(Z - P_{T^\perp}(Z))\|_F^2$$

$$= \|R_\Omega(P_{T^\perp}(Z))\|_F^2 \leq \|P_{T^\perp}(Z)\|_F^2$$

where in the last line we used that Z is supported in $\overline{\Omega}$, and so $R_\Omega(Z) = 0$. Hence we have that

$$\|P_{T^\perp}(Z)\|_F^2 \geq \frac{m}{n^2}\|P_T(Z)\|_F^2 - \frac{m}{2n^2}\|Z\|_F^2.$$

We can use the fact that $\|Z\|_F^2 = \|P_{T^\perp}(Z)\|_F^2 + \|P_T(Z)\|_F^2$ and conclude that $\|P_{T^\perp}(Z)\|_F^2 \geq \frac{m}{4n^2}\|P_T(Z)\|_F^2$. Now

$$\|P_{T^\perp}(Z)\|_*^2 \geq \|P_{T^\perp}(Z)\|_F^2 \geq \frac{m}{4n^2}\|P_T(Z)\|_F^2$$
$$> \frac{r}{2n}\|P_T(Z)\|_F^2$$

which completes the proof of the lemma. ∎

All that remains is to prove that the helper matrix Y that we made use of actually does exist (with high probability). Recall that we require that Y is supported in Ω and $\|P_T(Y) - UV^T\|_F \leq \sqrt{r/8n}$ and $\|P_{T^\perp}(Y)\| \leq 1/2$. The basic idea is to break up Ω into disjoint sets $\Omega_1, \Omega_2, \dots \Omega_p$, where $p = \log n$, and use each set of observations to make progress on the remaining $P_T(Y) - UV^T$. More precisely, initialize $Y_0 = 0$, in which case the remainder is $W_0 = UV^T$. Then set

$$Y_{i+1} = Y_i + \frac{n^2}{m}R_{\Omega_{i+1}}(W_i)$$

and update $W_{i+1} = UV^T - P_T(Y_{i+1})$. It is easy to see that $\mathbb{E}[\frac{n^2}{m}R_{\Omega_{i+1}}] = I$. Intuitively, this means that at each step $Y_{i+1} - Y_i$ is an unbiased estimator for W_i, and so we should expect the remainder to decrease quickly (here we will rely on the concentration bounds we derived from the noncommutative Bernstein inequality). Now we can explain the nomenclature *quantum golfing*: at each step, we hit our golf ball in the direction of the hole, but here our target is to approximate the matrix UV^T, which for various reasons is the type of question that arises in quantum mechanics.

It is easy to see that $Y = \sum_i Y_i$ is supported in Ω and that $P_T(W_i) = W_i$ for all i. Hence we can compute

$$\|P_T(Y_i) - UV^T\|_F = \left\| P_T\frac{n^2}{m}R_{\Omega_i}W_{i-1} - W_{i-1} \right\|_F$$
$$= \left\| P_T\frac{n^2}{m}R_{\Omega_i}P_TW_{i-1} - P_TW_{i-1} \right\|_F$$
$$= \frac{n^2}{m}\left\| P_TR_\Omega P_T - \frac{m}{n^2}P_T \right\|\|W_{i-1}\|_F \leq \frac{1}{2}\|W_{i-1}\|_F$$

where the last inequality follows from Lemma 8.3.3. Therefore, the Frobenius norm of the remainder decreases geometrically, and it is easy to guarantee that Y satisfies condition (a).

The more technically involved part is showing that Y also satisfies condition (b). However, the intuition is that $\|P_{T^\perp}(Y_1)\|$ is itself not too large, and since the norm of the remainder W_i decreases geometrically, we should expect that $\|P_{T^\perp}(Y_i)\|$ does too, and so most of the contribution to

$$\|P_{T^\perp}(Y)\| \leq \sum_i \|P_{T^\perp}(Y_i)\|$$

comes from the first term. For full details, see [123]. This completes the proof that computing the solution to the convex program indeed finds M *exactly*, provided that M is incoherent and $|\Omega| \geq \max(\mu_1^2, \mu_0)r(n+m)\log^2(n+m)$.

Further Remarks

There are many other approaches to matrix completion. What makes the above argument so technically involved is that we wanted to solve exact matrix completion. When our goal is to recover an approximation to M, it becomes much easier to show bounds on the performance of (P_1). Srebro and Shraibman [132] used Rademacher complexity and matrix concentration bounds to show that (P_1) recovers a solution that is close to M. Moreover, their argument extends straightforwardly to the arguably more practically relevant case when M is only entrywise close to being low-rank. Jain et al. [93] and Hardt [83] gave provable guarantees for alternating minimization. These guarantees are worse in terms of their dependence on the coherence, rank, and condition number of M, but alternating minimization has much better running time and space complexity and is the most popular approach in practice. Barak and Moitra [26] studied noisy tensor completion and showed that it is possible to complete tensors better than naively flattening them into matrices, and showed lower bounds based on the hardness of refuting random constraint satisfaction problems.

Following the work on matrix completion, convex programs have proven to be useful in many other related problems, such as separating a matrix into the sum of a low-rank and a sparse part [44]. Chandrasekaran et al. [46] gave a general framework for analyzing convex programs for linear inverse problems and applied it in many settings. An interesting direction is to use reductions and convex programming hierarchies as a framework for exploring computational versus statistical trade-offs [29, 45, 24].

Bibliography

[1] D. Achlioptas and F. McSherry. On spectral learning of mixtures of distributions. In *COLT*, pages 458–469, 2005.

[2] A. Agarwal, A. Anandkumar, P. Jain, P. Netrapalli, and R. Tandon. Learning sparsely used overcomplete dictionaries via alternating minimization. *arXiv:1310.7991*, 2013.

[3] A. Agarwal, A. Anandkumar, and P. Netrapalli. Exact recovery of sparsely used overcomplete dictionaries. *arXiv:1309.1952*, 2013.

[4] M. Aharon. Overcomplete dictionaries for sparse representation of signals. PhD thesis, 2006.

[5] M. Aharon, M. Elad, and A. Bruckstein. K-SVD: An algorithm for designing overcomplete dictionaries for sparse representation. *IEEE Trans. Signal Process.* 54(11):4311–4322, 2006.

[6] R. Ahlswede and A. Winter. Strong converse for identification via quantum channels. *IEEE Trans. Inf. Theory*, 48(3):569–579, 2002.

[7] N. Alon. Tools from higher algebra. In *Handbook of Combinatorics*, editors: R. L. Graham, M. Gr otschel, and L. Lovász. Cambridge, MA: MIT Press, 1996, pages 1749–1783.

[8] A. Anandkumar, D. Foster, D. Hsu, S. Kakade, and Y. Liu. A spectral algorithm for latent Dirichlet allocation. In *NIPS*, pages 926–934, 2012.

[9] A. Anandkumar, R. Ge, D. Hsu, and S. Kakade. A tensor spectral approach to learning mixed membership community models. In *COLT*, pages 867–881, 2013.

[10] A. Anandkumar, D. Hsu, and S. Kakade. A method of moments for hidden Markov models and multi-view mixture models. In *COLT*, pages 33.1–33.34, 2012.

[11] J. Anderson, M. Belkin, N. Goyal, L Rademacher, and J. Voss. The more the merrier: The blessing of dimensionality for learning large Gaussian mixtures. *arXiv:1311.2891*, 2013.

[12] S. Arora, R. Ge, Y. Halpern, D. Mimno, A. Moitra, D. Sontag, Y. Wu, and M. Zhu. A practical algorithm for topic modeling with provable guarantees. In *ICML*, pages 280–288, 2013.

[13] S. Arora, R. Ge, R. Kannan, and A. Moitra. Computing a nonnegative matrix factorization – provably. In *STOC*, pages 145–162, 2012.

[14] S. Arora, R. Ge, and A. Moitra. Learning topic models – going beyond SVD. In *FOCS*, pages 1–10, 2012.

[15] S. Arora, R. Ge, and A. Moitra. New algorithms for learning incoherent and overcomplete dictionaries. *arXiv:1308.6273*, 2013.

[16] S. Arora, R. Ge, T. Ma, and A. Moitra. Simple, efficient, and neural algorithms for sparse coding. In *COLT*, pages 113–149, 2015.

[17] S. Arora, R. Ge, A. Moitra, and S. Sachdeva. Provable ICA with unknown Gaussian noise, and implications for Gaussian mixtures and autoencoders. In *NIPS*, pages 2384–2392, 2012.

[18] S. Arora, R. Ge, S. Sachdeva, and G. Schoenebeck. Finding overlapping communities in social networks: Towards a rigorous approach. In *EC*, 2012.

[19] S. Arora and R. Kannan. Learning mixtures of separated nonspherical Gaussians. *Ann. Appl. Probab.*, 15(1A):69–92, 2005.

[20] M. Balcan, A. Blum, and A. Gupta. Clustering under approximation stability. *J. ACM*, 60(2): 1–34, 2013.

[21] M. Balcan, A. Blum, and N. Srebro. On a theory of learning with similarity functions. *Mach. Learn.*, 72(1–2):89–112, 2008.

[22] M. Balcan, C. Borgs, M. Braverman, J. Chayes, and S.-H. Teng. Finding endogenously formed communities. In *SODA*, 2013.

[23] A. Bandeira, P. Rigollet, and J. Weed. Optimal rates of estimation for multi-reference alignment. *arXiv:1702.08546*, 2017.

[24] B. Barak, S. Hopkins, J. Kelner, P. Kothari, A. Moitra, and A. Potechin. A nearly tight sum-of-squares lower bound for the planted clique problem. In *FOCS*, pages 428–437, 2016.

[25] B. Barak, J. Kelner, and D. Steurer. Dictionary learning and tensor decomposition via the sum-of-squares method. In *STOC*, pages 143–151, 2015.

[26] B. Barak and A. Moitra. Noisy tensor completion via the sum-of-squares hierarchy. In *COLT*, pages 417–445, 2016.

[27] M. Belkin and K. Sinha. Toward learning Gaussian mixtures with arbitrary separation. In *COLT*, pages 407–419, 2010.

[28] M. Belkin and K. Sinha. Polynomial learning of distribution families. In *FOCS*, pages 103–112, 2010.

[29] Q. Berthet and P. Rigollet. Complexity theoretic lower bounds for sparse principal component detection. In *COLT*, pages 1046–1066, 2013.

[30] A. Bhaskara, M. Charikar, and A. Vijayaraghavan. Uniqueness of tensor decompositions with applications to polynomial identifiability. In *COLT*, pages 742–778, 2014.

[31] A. Bhaskara, M. Charikar, A. Moitra, and A. Vijayaraghavan. Smoothed analysis of tensor decompositions. In *STOC*, pages 594–603, 2014.

[32] Y. Bilu and N. Linial. Are stable instances easy? *In Combinatorics, Probability and Computing*, 21(5):643–660, 2012.

[33] V. Bittorf, B. Recht, C. Re, and J. Tropp. Factoring nonnegative matrices with linear programs. In *NIPS*, 2012.

[34] D. Blei. Introduction to probabilistic topic models. *Commun. ACM*, 55(4):77–84, 2012.

[35] D. Blei and J. Lafferty. A correlated topic model of science. *Ann. Appl. Stat.*, 1(1):17–35, 2007.

[36] D. Blei, A. Ng, and M. Jordan. Latent Dirichlet allocation. *J. Mach. Learn. Res.*, 3:993–1022, 2003.

[37] A. Blum, A. Kalai, and H. Wasserman. Noise-tolerant learning, the parity problem, and the statistical query model. *J. ACM*, 50:506–519, 2003.

[38] A. Blum and J. Spencer. Coloring random and semi-random k-colorable graphs. *Journal of Algorithms*, 19(2):204–234, 1995.

[39] K. Borgwardt. *The Simplex Method: A Probabilistic Analysis*. New York: Springer, 2012.

[40] S. C. Brubaker and S. Vempala. Isotropic PCA and affine-invariant clustering. In *FOCS*, pages 551–560, 2008.

[41] E. Candes and B. Recht. Exact matrix completion via convex optimization. *Found. Comput. Math.*, 9(6):717–772, 2008.

[42] E. Candes, J. Romberg, and T. Tao. Stable signal recovery from incomplete and inaccurate measurements. *Comm. Pure Appl. Math.*, 59(8):1207–1223, 2006.

[43] E. Candes and T. Tao. Decoding by linear programming. *IEEE Trans. Inf. Theory*, 51(12):4203–4215, 2005.

[44] E. Candes, X. Li, Y. Ma, and J. Wright. Robust principal component analysis? *J. ACM*, 58(3):1–37, 2011.

[45] V. Chandrasekaran and M. Jordan. Computational and statistical tradeoffs via convex relaxation. *Proc. Natl. Acad. Sci. U.S.A.*, 110(13):E1181–E1190, 2013.

[46] V. Chandrasekaran, B. Recht, P. Parrilo, and A. Willsky. The convex geometry of linear inverse problems. *Found. Comput. Math.*, 12(6):805–849, 2012.

[47] J. Chang. Full reconstruction of Markov models on evolutionary trees: Identifiability and consistency. *Math. Biosci.*, 137(1):51–73, 1996.

[48] K. Chaudhuri and S. Rao. Learning mixtures of product distributions using correlations and independence. In *COLT*, pages 9–20, 2008.

[49] K. Chaudhuri and S. Rao. Beyond Gaussians: Spectral methods for learning mixtures of heavy-tailed distributions. In *COLT*, pages 21–32, 2008.

[50] S. Chen, D. Donoho, and M. Saunders. Atomic decomposition by basis pursuit. *SIAM J. Sci. Comput.*, 20(1):33–61, 1998.

[51] A. Cohen, W. Dahmen, and R. DeVore. Compressed sensing and best k-term approximation. *J. AMS*, 22(1):211–231, 2009.

[52] J. Cohen and U. Rothblum. Nonnegative ranks, decompositions and factorizations of nonnegative matrices. *Linear Algebra Appl.*, 190:149–168, 1993.

[53] P. Comon. Independent component analysis: A new concept? *Signal Processing*, 36(3):287–314, 1994.

[54] A. Dasgupta. *Asymptotic Theory of Statistics and Probability*. New York: Springer, 2008.

[55] A. Dasgupta, J. Hopcroft, J. Kleinberg, and M. Sandler. On learning mixtures of heavy-tailed distributions. In *FOCS*, pages 491–500, 2005.

[56] S. Dasgupta. Learning mixtures of Gaussians. In *FOCS*, pages 634–644, 1999.

[57] S. Dasgupta and L. J. Schulman. A two-round variant of EM for Gaussian mixtures. In *UAI*, pages 152–159, 2000.

[58] G. Davis, S. Mallat, and M. Avellaneda. Greedy adaptive approximations. *Constr. Approx.*, 13:57–98, 1997.

[59] L. De Lathauwer, J Castaing, and J. Cardoso. Fourth-order cumulant-based blind identification of underdetermined mixtures. *IEEE Trans. Signal Process.*, 55(6):2965–2973, 2007.

[60] S. Deerwester, S. Dumais, T. Landauer, G. Furnas, and R. Harshman. Indexing by latent semantic analysis. *J. Assoc. Inf. Sci. Technol.*, 41(6):391–407, 1990.

[61] A. P. Dempster, N. M. Laird, and D. B. Rubin. Maximum likelihood from incomplete data via the EM algorithm. *J. R. Stat. Soc. Series B Stat. Methodol.*, 39(1):1–38, 1977.

[62] D. Donoho and M. Elad. Optimally sparse representation in general (non-orthogonal) dictionaries via ℓ_1-minimization. *Proc. Natl. Acad. Sci. U.S.A.*, 100(5):2197–2202, 2003.

[63] D. Donoho and X. Huo. Uncertainty principles and ideal atomic decomposition. *IEEE Trans. Inf. Theory*, 47(7):2845–2862, 1999.

[64] D. Donoho and P. Stark. Uncertainty principles and signal recovery. *SIAM J. Appl. Math.*, 49(3):906–931, 1989.

[65] D. Donoho and V. Stodden. When does nonnegative matrix factorization give the correct decomposition into parts? In *NIPS*, 2003.

[66] R. Downey and M. Fellows. *Parameterized Complexity*. New York: Springer, 2012.

[67] M. Elad. *Sparse and Redundant Representations*. New York: Springer, 2010.

[68] K. Engan, S. Aase, and J. Hakon-Husoy. Method of optimal directions for frame design. *Proc. IEEE Int. Conf. Acoust. Speech Signal Process.*, 5:2443–2446, 1999.

[69] P. Erdos, M. Steel, L. Szekely, and T. Warnow. A few logs suffice to build (almost) all trees. I. *Random Struct. Algorithms*, 14:153–184, 1997.

[70] M. Fazel. Matrix rank minimization with applications. PhD thesis, Stanford University, 2002.

[71] U. Feige and J. Kilian. Heuristics for semirandom graph problems. *J. Comput. Syst. Sci.*, 63(4):639–671, 2001.

[72] U. Feige and R. Krauthgamer. Finding and certifying a large hidden clique in a semirandom graph. *Random Struct. Algorithms*, 16(2):195–208, 2009.

[73] J. Feldman, R. A. Servedio, and R. O'Donnell. PAC learning axis-aligned mixtures of Gaussians with no separation assumption. In *COLT*, pages 20–34, 2006.

[74] A. Frieze, M. Jerrum, and R. Kannan. Learning linear transformations. In *FOCS*, pages 359–368, 1996.

[75] A. Garnaev and E. Gluskin. The widths of a Euclidean ball. *Sov. Math. Dokl.*, 277(5):200–204, 1984.

[76] R. Ge and T. Ma. Decomposing overcomplete 3rd order tensors using sum-of-squares algorithms. In *RANDOM*, pages 829–849, 2015.

[77] A. Gilbert, S. Muthukrishnan, and M. Strauss. Approximation of functions over redundant dictionaries using coherence. In *SODA*, pages 243–252, 2003.

[78] N. Gillis. Robustness analysis of hotttopixx, a linear programming model for factoring nonnegative matrices. *arXiv:1211.6687*, 2012.

[79] N. Goyal, S. Vempala, and Y. Xiao. Fourier PCA. In *STOC*, pages 584–593, 2014.

[80] D. Gross. Recovering low-rank matrices from few coefficients in any basis. *arXiv:0910.1879*, 2009.

[81] D. Gross, Y.-K. Liu, S. Flammia, S. Becker, and J. Eisert. Quantum state tomography via compressed sensing. *Phys. Rev. Lett.*, 105(15):150401, 2010.

[82] V. Guruswami, J. Lee, and A. Razborov. Almost Euclidean subspaces of ℓ_1^n via expander codes. *Combinatorica*, 30(1):47–68, 2010.

[83] M. Hardt. Understanding alternating minimization for matrix completion. In *FOCS*, pages 651–660, 2014.

[84] R. Harshman. Foundations of the PARAFAC procedure: model and conditions for an "explanatory" multi-mode factor analysis. *UCLA Working Papers in Phonetics*, 16:1–84, 1970.

[85] J. Håstad. Tensor rank is *NP*-complete. *J. Algorithms*, 11(4):644–654, 1990.

[86] C. Hillar and L.-H. Lim. Most tensor problems are *NP*-hard. *arXiv:0911.1393v4*, 2013

[87] T. Hofmann. Probabilistic latent semantic analysis. In *UAI*, pages 289–296, 1999.

[88] R. Horn and C. Johnson. *Matrix Analysis*. New York: Cambridge University Press, 1990.

[89] D. Hsu and S. Kakade. Learning mixtures of spherical Gaussians: Moment methods and spectral decompositions. In *ITCS*, pages 11–20, 2013.

[90] P. J. Huber. Projection pursuit. *Ann. Stat.*, 13:435–475, 1985.

[91] R. A. Hummel and B. C. Gidas. Zero crossings and the heat equation. Courant Institute of Mathematical Sciences, TR-111, 1984.

[92] R. Impagliazzo and R. Paturi. On the complexity of k-SAT. *J. Comput. Syst. Sci.*, 62(2):367–375, 2001.

[93] P. Jain, P. Netrapalli, and S. Sanghavi. Low rank matrix completion using alternating minimization. In *STOC*, pages 665–674, 2013.

[94] A. T. Kalai, A. Moitra, and G. Valiant. Efficiently learning mixtures of two Gaussians. In *STOC*, pages 553–562, 2010.

[95] R. Karp. Probabilistic analysis of some combinatorial search problems. In *Algorithms and Complexity: New Directions and Recent Results*. New York: Academic Press, 1976, pages 1–19.

[96] B. Kashin and V. Temlyakov. A remark on compressed sensing. Manuscript, 2007.

[97] L. Khachiyan. On the complexity of approximating extremal determinants in matrices. *J. Complexity*, 11(1):138–153, 1995.

[98] D. Koller and N. Friedman. *Probabilistic Graphical Models*. Cambridge, MA: MIT Press, 2009.

[99] J. Kruskal. Three-way arrays: Rank and uniqueness of trilinear decompositions with applications to arithmetic complexity and statistics. *Linear Algebra Appl.*, 18(2):95–138, 1997.

[100] A. Kumar, V. Sindhwani, and P. Kambadur. Fast conical hull algorithms for near-separable non-negative matrix factorization. In *ICML*, pages 231–239, 2013.

[101] D. Lee and H. Seung. Learning the parts of objects by non-negative matrix factorization. *Nature*, 401(6755):788-791, 1999.

[102] D. Lee and H. Seung. Algorithms for non-negative matrix factorization. In *NIPS*, pages 556–562, 2000.

[103] S. Leurgans, R. Ross, and R. Abel. A decomposition for three-way arrays. *SIAM J. Matrix Anal. Appl.*, 14(4):1064–1083, 1993.

[104] M. Lewicki and T. Sejnowski. Learning overcomplete representations. *Comput.*, 12:337–365, 2000.

[105] W. Li and A. McCallum. Pachinko allocation: DAG-structured mixture models of topic correlations. In *ICML*, pp. 633-640, 2007.

[106] B. Lindsay. *Mixture Models: Theory, Geometry and Applications*. Hayward, CA: Institute for Mathematical Statistics, 1995.

[107] B. F. Logan. Properties of high-pass signals. PhD thesis, Columbia University, 1965.

[108] L. Lovász and M. Saks. Communication complexity and combinatorial lattice theory. *J. Comput. Syst. Sci.*, 47(2):322–349, 1993.

[109] F. McSherry. Spectral partitioning of random graphs. In *FOCS*, pages 529–537, 2001.

[110] S. Mallat. *A Wavelet Tour of Signal Processing*. New York: Academic Press, 1998.

[111] S. Mallat and Z. Zhang. Matching pursuits with time-frequency dictionaries. *IEEE Trans. Signal Process.*, 41(12):3397–3415, 1993.

[112] A. Moitra. An almost optimal algorithm for computing nonnegative rank. In *SODA*, pages 1454–1464, 2013.

[113] A. Moitra. Super-resolution, extremal functions and the condition number of Vandermonde matrices. In *STOC*, pages 821–830, 2015.

[114] A. Moitra and G. Valiant. Setting the polynomial learnability of mixtures of Gaussians. In *FOCS*, pages 93–102, 2010.

[115] E. Mossel and S. Roch. Learning nonsingular phylogenies and hidden Markov models. In *STOC*, pages 366–375, 2005.

[116] Y. Nesterov. *Introductory Lectures on Convex Optimization: A Basic Course*. New York: Springer, 2004.

[117] B. Olshausen and B. Field. Sparse coding with an overcomplete basis set: A strategy employed by V1? *Vision Research*, 37(23):3311–3325, 1997.

[118] C. Papadimitriou, P. Raghavan, H. Tamaki, and S. Vempala. Latent semantic indexing: A probabilistic analysis. *J. Comput. Syst. Sci.*, 61(2):217–235, 2000.

[119] Y. Pati, R. Rezaiifar, and P. Krishnaprasad. Orthogonal matching pursuit: Recursive function approximation with applications to wavelet decomposition. *Asilomar Conference on Signals, Systems, and Computers*, pages 40–44, 1993.

[120] K. Pearson. Contributions to the mathematical theory of evolution. *Philos. Trans. Royal Soc. A*, 185: 71–110, 1894.

[121] Y. Rabani, L. Schulman, and C. Swamy. Learning mixtures of arbitrary distributions over large discrete domains. In *ITCS*, pages 207–224, 2014.

[122] R. Raz. Tensor-rank and lower bounds for arithmetic formulas. In *STOC*, pages 659–666, 2010.

[123] B. Recht. A simpler approach to matrix completion. *J. Mach. Learn. Res.*, 12:3413–3430, 2011.

[124] B. Recht, M. Fazel, and P. Parrilo. Guaranteed minimum rank solutions of matrix equations via nuclear norm minimization. *SIAM Rev.*, 52(3):471–501, 2010.

[125] R. A. Redner and H. F. Walker. Mixture densities, maximum likelihood and the EM algorithm. *SIAM Rev.*, 26(2):195–239, 1984.

[126] J. Renegar. On the computational complexity and geometry of the first-order theory of the reals. *J. Symb. Comput.*, 13(1):255–352, 1991.

[127] T. Rockefellar. *Convex Analysis*. Princeton, NJ: Princeton University Press, 1996.

[128] A. Seidenberg. A new decision method for elementary algebra. *Ann. Math.*, 60(2):365–374, 1954.

[129] V. de Silva and L.-H. Lim. Tensor rank and the ill-posedness of the best low rank approximation problem. *SIAM J. Matrix Anal. Appl.*, 30(3):1084–1127, 2008.

[130] D. Spielman and S.-H. Teng. Smoothed analysis of algorithms: Why the simplex algorithm usually takes polynomial time. In *Journal of the ACM*, 51(3):385–463, 2004.

[131] D. Spielman, H. Wang, and J. Wright. Exact recovery of sparsely-used dictionaries. *J. Mach. Learn. Res.*, 23:1–18, 2012.

[132] N. Srebro and A. Shraibman. Rank, trace-norm and max-norm. In *COLT*, pages 545–560, 2005.

[133] M. Steel. Recovering a tree from the leaf colourations it generates under a Markov model. *Appl. Math. Lett.*, 7:19–24, 1994.

[134] A. Tarski. A decision method for elementary algebra and geometry. Berkeley and Los Angeles: University of California Press, 1951.

[135] H. Teicher. Identifiability of mixtures. *Ann. Math. Stat.*, 31(1):244–248, 1961.

[136] J. Tropp. Greed is good: Algorithmic results for sparse approximation. *IEEE Trans. Inf. Theory*, 50(10):2231–2242, 2004.

[137] J. Tropp, A. Gilbert, S. Muthukrishnan, and M. Strauss. Improved sparse approximation over quasi-incoherent dictionaries. *IEEE International Conference on Image Processing*, 1:37–40, 2003.

[138] L. Valiant. A theory of the learnable. *Commun. ACM*, 27(11):1134–1142, 1984.

[139] S. Vavasis. On the complexity of nonnegative matrix factorization. *SIAM J. Optim.*, 20(3):1364–1377, 2009.

[140] S. Vempala and Y. Xiao. Structure from local optima: Learning subspace juntas via higher order PCA. *arXiv:abs/1108.3329*, 2011.

[141] S. Vempala and G. Wang. A spectral algorithm for learning mixture models. *J. Comput. Syst. Sci.*, 68(4):841–860, 2004.

[142] M. Wainwright and M. Jordan. Graphical models, exponential families, and variational inference. *Foundations and Trends in Machine Learning*, 1(1–2): 1–305, 2008.

[143] P. Wedin. Perturbation bounds in connection with singular value decompositions. *BIT Numer. Math.*, 12:99–111, 1972.

[144] M. Yannakakis. Expressing combinatorial optimization problems by linear programs. *J. Comput. Syst. Sci.*, 43(3):441–466, 1991.

Index